# TRANSNATIONAL
# LEADERSHIP
# DEVELOPMENT

# TRANSNATIONAL LEADERSHIP DEVELOPMENT

Preparing the Next Generation
for the Borderless Business World

Beth Fisher-Yoshida, Ph.D.

Kathy D. Geller, Ph.D.

American Management Association

New York • Atlanta • Brussels • Chicago • Mexico City
San Francisco • Shanghai • Tokyo • Toronto • Washington, D. C.

This publication is designed to provide accurate and authoritative information in regard to the subject matter covered. It is sold with the understanding that the publisher is not engaged in rendering legal, accounting, or other professional service. If legal advice or other expert assistance is required, the services of a competent professional person should be sought.

Library of Congress Cataloging-in-Publication Data

Fisher-Yoshida, Beth.
    Transnational leadership development : preparing the next generation for the borderless business world / Beth Fisher-Yoshida and Kathy Geller.
        p.    cm.
    Includes bibliographical references and index.
    ISBN 978-0-8144-1039-4
    1. Leadership—Cross-cultural studies. 2. International business enterprises—Management. 3. Intercultural communication. 4. Corporate culture—Cross-cultural studies. I. Geller, Kathy Dee. II. Title.
    HD57.7.F5837 2009
    658.4′092—dc22
                                                                            2008033098

Printing number

10 9 8 7 6 5 4 3 2 1

# NEW FROM AMA

## The Adult Learning Theory and Practice Book Series

### ABOUT THE SERIES

This new book series is intended to provide new thinking about adult learning theory and practice and will serve as a bridge across professions, disciplines, geographical, and cultural boundaries. The **Adult Learning Theory and Practice Series** is designed to provide insights based on research for scholars and practitioners who help adults and organizations learn, develop, grow, and change. Each book in this series will address a new issue or theory in adult learning, identify relevant resources and practical tools for application, and present the results of new, original research that link theory and practice.

To learn more about the Adult Learning Theory and Practice Book Series, please contact the series editors or Jacqueline Flynn.

### SERIES EDITORS:

Dr. William J. Rothwell–(814) 863-2581; wjr9@psu.edu
Dr. Victoria J. Marsick–(212) 678-3754; Vmarsick@aol.com
Dr. Andrea D. Ellinger–(217) 333-0807; adelling@uiuc.edu
Ms. Jacqueline Flynn, Executive Editor, AMACOM Books
(212) 903-8379–jflynn@amanet.org

To find submission guidelines and learn more about the Adult Learning Theory and Practice series, please go to:
www.amanet.org/go/AMAInnovationsAdultLearning

# ADVISORY BOARD

**Bill Gardner** has worldwide responsibility for Executive Assessment, Executive & Leadership Development, Succession Planning, Learning & Collaborative Technologies, Performance Management, Corporate Learning & Development, and Organization Development for Advanced Micro Devices (AMD). Under Bill's leadership AMD's Learning & Development organization was named to *Training* magazine's Top 100 learning & education groups in 2001, 2002, 2003 and 2004. He holds a BS in Finance from Mississippi State and an MBA from the University of Southern Mississippi.

**Dave Medrano** is an Associate Dean for the corporate university of one of the world's leading multinational automotive companies where he directs training and development to support sales and marketing functions. He is also responsible for reconfiguring training programs for the company's global workforce. He speaks internationally to industry groups and holds a B.A. from the University of California at Los Angeles and an MBA from Pepperdine University.

**Rich Wellins, Ph.D.** is a Senior Vice President with Development Dimensions International (DDI) where his responsibilities include leading the Center for Applied Behavioral Research, developing and launching a new leadership development system, and building systems for internal knowledge management. He is a frequent speaker and has written 6 books, including the best seller *Empowered Teams*. He holds a Doctorate in social/industrial psychology from American University.

# EDITORIAL BOARD

# ABOUT THE AUTHORS

## Beth Fisher-Yoshida

Dr. Beth Fisher-Yoshida, the founder and Managing Director of FYI Fisher Yoshida International, LLC, is an organizational development consultant, facilitator, corporate trainer, mediator, and executive coach, who partners with clients to develop customized interventions aimed at improving organizational performance as well as professional and personal development. Clients have included organizations in the Fortune 100, private, not-for-profit, and government sectors in the United States, Canada, Asia, Europe, Africa, and the Middle East. They include NASA, the United Nations, and academic institutions, such as Columbia University. Their specialties range from finance to pharmaceutical goods, consumer goods, human rights, and education.

One main focus of Dr. Fisher-Yoshida's work is addressing intercultural competence and diversity, as well as performance issues and conflicts influenced by worldview differences. With more than 20 years experience and 13 years living in Japan, she assists client organizations to support their efforts for change through leadership development; conflict resolution management systems, negotiation, and mediation; intercultural communication and diversity; team development and effectiveness; and performance management. In addition to consulting, Dr. Fisher- Yoshida is Academic Director of the new Master of Science in Negotiation and Conflict Resolution at Columbia University in New York City. She is also on the faculty in the Social and Organizational Psychology program at Teachers College and in the School of Continuing Education, both at Columbia University. Dr. Fisher-Yoshida researches and publishes articles and chapters on self-awareness, cultural competency, leadership development, and conflict resolution. For more information please see www.fyicommunicate.com .

## Kathy D. Geller

Dr. Kathy Geller is presently Director of Organizational Effectiveness at Stanford University, a position she accepted after five years as Managing Director of Areté Leadership International Limited, an international consultancy focused on supporting business performance through leadership development. Working in Asia for the last 10 years, Dr. Geller brings expertise in merging the business orientation of the West with an understanding and appreciation of the relational aspects of the East. Through her work with Areté Leadership International, she supported the development of executives, leaders, and managers in the talent pipeline of Fortune 100 U.S. and European multinationals with a significant presence in Asia. Recognizing the paradoxes inherent within their settings provides these leaders with a process and the tools to lead more effectively.

Before establishing Areté Leadership International Limited, Kathy was Chief Curriculum Architect for Personal and Managerial Effectiveness and Global Head of Management Development for Standard Chartered Bank, a 70,000-person British financial services organization serving Asia, Africa, and the Middle East. Based in Hong Kong, Dr. Geller and her team supported the organization's growth and change by creating learning interventions aligned to business strategy, organization values, and cognizance of transnational needs.

Dr. Geller is also an instructor in Columbia University's Summer Principal's Academy, a master's level program focused on developing leadership talent for urban roles in education. In addition to her work at Columbia University, Dr. Geller is an adjunct professor with Nova Southeastern University's teaching Leadership, Change Leadership, and Communications at the Doctoral level. Based in Asia, she taught "Leadership" and "Trend and Issues" to Southeast Asian and Northeast Asian Cohorts of international educators, and she also teaches in the United States in an on-line environment.

Whether in corporate settings or graduate classrooms, Dr. Geller believes that the leaders of today need to be accomplished at effectively engaging others, responding flexibly to complex social, political, and economic changes, and leading with a strong knowledge of one's strengths as well as an appropriate sense of appreciation for others; Kathy draws from adult learning theory using experiential and conversational processes to broaden and transform ways of thinking and acting. For more information, go to www.areteleadership.com.

American Management Association
www.amanet.org

# CONTENTS

A link to the survey developed by the authors for *Transnational Leadership Development* can be found at:
http://www.surveymonkey.com/s.aspx?sm=oVV9Pv72H2_2fbxXd
PJJnLiQ_3d_3d

# FOREWORD

"Electrons don't have culture!" an engineer protested recently during a corporate training program. "Scientists think the same all over the world; it's just logic and reason."

Ah, I thought, but *whose* logic and reason?

And therein lies one of the questions at the core of globalization. Whose values, whose thinking patterns, whose communication styles, whose negotiation model will shape our interactions?

The answers are no longer quite so simple as they may have been in past decades, when we might possibly have survived assuming that culture-free electrons truly eradicated the complexity of human interaction. As the Workforce 2020 report notes, these days, "the rest of the world matters" (Judy & D'Amico, 1997).[1]

This book is an acknowledgement of that reality, and an invitation to enjoy all of the possibilities a vast and intriguing world of differences can bring. By deliberately avoiding the tired—and tiring—perspective that intercultural partnerships are fraught with "problems," the authors have presented a fresh view of cultural contrasts that provides a window to explore one's culture, and that of others. For the manager seeking to understand why an interview went awry, for the virtual team members wondering why the work isn't getting done, for employees hoping we can "all just get along," and for ourselves, pondering where our culture fits in the world, this text offers a practical introduction to cultural values, beliefs, and behaviors.

The authors' wide range of experiences in other cultures, particularly in Asia, lend an important vantage point for this exploration, highlighting the subtleties of unspoken meanings that many of us find so elusive. The multi-cultural perspectives they bring to the analysis enrich many of the dilemmas they illustrate.

They share the current view in the field that leadership is not confined to the person at the top of the flow chart; leadership is more than position power. With dynamic and interconnected work worlds, "leadership" takes on a new meaning, with the implication that each of us shares responsibility for our interactions across borders and boundaries. Intercultural competence is not merely the purview of senior executives, but must be reflected throughout all levels and functions of the organization.

The engineer might say "But if you know your job, that's all that matters—the rest will follow!" The realistic and multifaceted case studies in each chapter demonstrate that this is wishful thinking, a soothing but often ineffective approach to cultural exchanges. Knowledge of our own profession, the authors suggest, does not equal competence in other cultures!

And so, while the electrons may not have culture, the engineers who talk about them certainly do. This book prepares us for that interface, and for the inevitable future of what educator Maxine Green calls "a world lived in common with others."[2] The future is upon us, and it is intriguing!

*Janet M. Bennett, Ph.D.*
*Executive Director*
*Intercultural Communication Institute*
*Portland, OR*

1. Judy, R. W., & D'Amico, C. (1997). *Workforce 2020: Work and workers in the 21st century.* Indianapolis, IN: Hudson Institute.
2. Green, M. (1988). *Dialectic of Freedom.* New York: Teachers College Press.

# PREFACE

*We are all transnational leaders in today's world. . . .*

The five paradoxes of transnational leadership are about living and leading effectively in today's world—a global village. It's about letting go of our expectations or desire for sameness and accepting that our effectiveness with others can be enhanced by knowing, honoring, and welcoming difference. It is in our best interest to approach others who are not like us with an air of curiosity and openness to the potential of what could be.

In the 20th century, the United States described itself as a "melting pot" expecting those who came into contact with its culture to melt into the mélange thinking, acting, speaking, and feeling in an agreed way. Assimilation into the American way of life was promoted over maintaining different cultural traditions. For much of the century, the British, Dutch, French, Portuguese, other European countries, and Japan took a colonialist perspective, educating those within their spheres of control and influence to understand, acknowledge, and imitate their cultures. Difference was to be ignored.

During part of this same period, China's doors were closed to the West. Difference was negated.

Over the recent twenty-five years, we are seeing the balance of economic power and the basis for wealth extend beyond the West into Asia and the Middle East. Technology created first to simplify work has in fact networked the world, diminishing distance and boundaries and creating relationships where none previously existed. It is in this setting of shifting power bases, changing economic tides and global integration that difference becomes something to embrace rather than deny or disparage. Embracing difference means we need to know ourselves, learn about others, and honor them as they are, not as we wish them to be.

As we embrace difference, we come to realize that while we are all "human beings," our way of *being* is in fact influenced by the cultural experiences that create our frames of reference and our beliefs. While the external trappings of this global world (dress, transport, homes, entertainment) are increasingly the same, it becomes ever more important to value different points of view and ways of experiencing the world. Now, more than ever before, to be successful in our lives and our work as transnational leaders, we need to recognize the importance of diversity as a key factor for our success. Each of us must develop an awareness of the paradoxes that thwart our best intentions in communicating and working effectively with others. For, it is in this awareness that trust and respect will flourish.

## WHAT DOES IT MEAN TO BE
## A TRANSNATIONAL LEADER?

As the business world becomes increasingly borderless, leaders and managers of all cultures are being called upon with greater frequency to assume leadership roles in other countries or with diverse multicultural teams in their own countries. Whatever our culture of origin, each person leading transnationally has to learn new ways of understanding themselves and experiencing difference, all the while maintaining a willingness to keep learning and deepening their knowledge of the present context.

Our initial and continued success as transnational leaders in other cultures or with those of other cultures is not just about our adapting to where they are or, conversely, expecting others to adapt to where we are. Successful transnational leaders understand that our success depends on developing new knowledge and new skills in managing the paradoxes of relationship and communication that we will face. Being an effective transnational leader requires the ability to see, feel, and experience the world with a different focus, communicating in new ways, being resilient, and taking time to reflect on what we know and need to learn.

## WHO IS THE INTENDED AUDIENCE
## FOR THIS BOOK?

Our purpose in writing this book is to assist people across the world to recognize and honor the differences we are all experiencing at increasing rates of frequency and depths of pervasiveness. We assume that in our normal interactions in today's world, we are regularly communicating with those from other cultures. While we have entitled the book *"Transnational Leadership,"* leadership, as we use it here, may be as much about leading ourselves as it is about leading others. Hence, no matter our position or role in today's world, we may find building our understanding of the paradoxes helpful.

As a part of *The Adult Learning Theory and Practice Series: Crossroads in Adult Learning,* this book is written for practitioners who work in this world of global diversity and for those who "facilitate, manage and support adult learning in the workplace and organizational settings," as well as in a range of educational settings. It is our purpose to support "the growing importance of (and impact of) globalization . . . the need for understanding of differences in how adults take in and interpret information, acquire skills, build knowledge, and use what they know. . . . Adult learning is inextricably intertwined with the learning of others: in groups, communities, networks, organizations, institutions and social settings" (Ellinger, Marsick, & Rothwell, 2005). We believe this book offers a basis for the design of learning interventions aimed at developing understanding, tolerance, and acceptance of cultural difference that will improve the effectiveness of individuals and assure the sustainability of organizations in today and tomorrow's world.

## OUR RESEARCH

Over the past ten years we have personally worked with over 5,000 leaders in multinational corporations, world agencies, and educational settings across the world designing and facilitating learning in Asia, Africa, the Middle East, Europe, and the Americas. In workshops and through coaching executives, managers and adult students seeking graduate education, we sought to fully understand the challenges faced by these transnational leaders and then to identify and understand the paradoxes embraced by those who were successful, as well as those who continued to find it challenging.

Building on what we saw, heard, and experienced in our work, as scholar-practitioners we then drew from the theory and research of transformational leadership, cross-cultural communication, and adult learning to create learning approaches designed specifically to develop leaders and managers working transnationally. During this time, we have individually and together designed and facilitated these programs in China, Japan, Southeast Asia, India, Kenya, Ghana, Botswana, Zimbabwe, and South Africa, as well as in the United States and Europe. Drawing on what we learned from those who shared their lives, challenged their approaches, and developed their effectiveness, we offer to you these insights in this book. The case studies we present, the stories we tell, and the conversations we have with the reader have their foundation in these streams of theory, research, and practice of transformational leadership, intercultural communication, and adult learning. Through our endnotes and references, you will become aware of those whose work provided a foundation for our own.

We have designed a survey based on these five paradoxes for which we are currently collecting data to establish global norms. There is information in the back of the book directing you to the Web site so that you, too, can see where you are with colleagues from around the world. The results will show you your strengths and suggest strategies and techniques for what you might do differently to enhance your effectiveness. Thank you for participating!

## OUR PRACTICE

We would be remiss, if we did not offer the reader an understanding of our own experiences in dealing with these paradoxes. Beth lived and worked in Japan for thirteen years working with one of the world's leading international management consultancies providing learning, development, and intercultural consulting to both global and Japanese companies. Kathy has lived in Asia for the last ten years and, during this time, led the management development function for a 70,000-person British financial services organization focused on operations in Asia, Africa, and the Middle East from a base in Hong Kong, serving as the chief curriculum architect for leadership development during her tenure. We both continue to work globally with diverse multicultural populations in our own consulting companies. Drawing from our personal experiences as well as from our professional views and research, we each bring a unique and lived perspective to our work, believing that it is the intersection of knowing and honoring ourselves and knowing and honoring others that frames the basis for effective relationships and enriched lives.

*Beth Fisher-Yoshida, Ph.D.*       *Kathy D. Geller, Ph.D.*
*New York, NY*                     *Palo Alto, CA*

December 2008

American Management Association
www.amanet.org

# 1 | INTRODUCTION

*I do not want my house to be walled in on all sides and my windows to be stuffed.*
*I want the cultures of all the lands to be blown about my house as freely as possible.*
*But I refuse to be blown off my feet by any.*

—MAHATMA GANDHI[1]

## CHANGING WORK STRUCTURES

It is difficult to walk past a section of business books today and not see the words international or global in the many titles on the shelves. The globalization heralded for more than 25 years has arrived and, with it, our experiences in working across borders and cultures is changing forever.

Advances in technology offer increased personal accessibility, and the traditional separation of our personal and professional lives is changing, as the boundaries between the two become less distinct than at any time in our experience. In the world of today work flows fluidly beyond the boundaries of the office. People communicate 24/7 on Blackberries™, I-phones™, and other personal communication devices; whole cities are now wired for mobile communication (wi-fi); and written and spoken communication access is seemingly endless and timeless.

As of result of these advances, the way business is conducted has been changing. The cumulative effect of these changes has impacted the ways in which leadership needs to be thought about and acted upon. In the networked world of today, organizations have open access to the human resources and talents of the world, and business alliances, employees, and clients are frequently drawn from borders beyond the corporate home country. In addition, as the populations of the developed regions retire (e.g., Japan, North America, Singapore, and Western Europe) and national birth rates are insufficient to provide an adequate pipeline of talent, new immigrant populations are arriving to take on key professional roles. The face of diversity in our workplace is rapidly increasing.

These changes herald a transformation from a *multinational* business model to a *transnational* model. Samuel Palmisano, Chairman and CEO of IBM, encourages a view of the corporation today as a "globally integrated enterprise," suggesting that by reframing our view from the multinational perspective (i.e., headquarter structures with minireplications around the globe) to a transnational context, our focus shifts from "products to production—from what things companies choose to make to how they choose to make them, from what services they offer to how they choose to deliver them."[2]

In this ever-evolving transnational environment,[3] organizations relocate jobs and people worldwide with the goal of "moving work to the places with the talent to handle the job and the time to do it at the right cost."[4] Work moves fluidly across borders and reporting lines reflect the transformed horizontal and global nature of business.

In these transnational settings, leaders may find that a team member who was previously in the next cubicle, the Systems Analyst they used to meet with on the eighth floor, the monthly budget review meeting with finance team held in the fifth floor conference room, or the conversation with the Georgia call center has shifted. Today, that team member is based in Singapore, the Systems Analyst is a member of an alliance partnership in Wales, the accounting function is outsourced to a vendor in Mexico City, and customer service is being done from a subsidiary in Bangalore. In this environment, the transnational leader is likely communicating with people and teams from multiple cultures and worldwide locales, and his or her ability to work successfully with these colleagues requires effective communication in a world that is truly diverse.

Unlike the multinational model of organization that assumed that everyone would assimilate to a specific set of values and beliefs drawn from a single culture, transnational organizations are recognizing the importance of diversity as a key factor in the ability of the organization to be sustainable and successful in the world of today. In this milieu, the paradox of working effectively across cultures becomes evident.

## THE CONFLUENCE OF THREE VARIABLES HAVE CREATED TRANSNATIONAL ORGANIZATIONS

Globalization, as we are now experiencing it, is based on the confluence of three variables:

- Deterritorialization
- Interconnectedness
- Speed of change

*Deterritorialization*[5] describes the manner in which cultural considerations are able to transcend territorial boundaries. It reflects the increasing number of social activities that take place among people regardless of the geographic locations of the participants. Nowhere is this more evident than in the rapid development of on-line social networks in the past 5 years: "Facebook™" and "YouTube™" are two of many popular examples of this. These on-line environments provide a platform for instantaneous, transnational interactions with both synchronous and asynchronous opportunities to share information and space and to work collaboratively.

This is similarly apparent in the increase of virtual work teams across the globe, where team members based in many different locations throughout the world work together on joint projects, sharing notes, diagrams, and conversations in virtual space and time. *Deterritorialization* supports the development of horizontal networks and brings together virtually the best people to get the job done.

A second key element of globalization is the significant *interconnectedness* of people, processes, systems, and organizations across the world, with the realization that decisions made in geographically distant locations impact local life. This phenomenon is evidenced when organizations reconfigure themselves from a collection of businesses, products, and country-based subsidiaries to a series of specialized functions that can be performed within the boundaries of the organization or outsourced to providers; these organizations can be located anywhere around the world to take advantage of local expertise and advantageous economic conditions.

The third critical element in this globalization is the *speed of change* in which these activities are taking place. As mentioned, technological advances allow for communication and a flow of information at ever-increasing speeds. Globalization, as we know it, has been occurring over the past two centuries, but it has taken a more intensive turn in recent years because of improvements and innovations in communication, transportation, and information technologies, and the speeds at which they are conducted. The impact of these changes is felt economically, politically, and culturally. Socially and culturally, globalization manifests itself in ways as ordinary as consumer-purchasing habits. Youth around the world today share tastes in music and clothing that are more similar than ever before. Financial transactions that move money across the world represent the economic evidence of globalization, and political movements gain momentum with support of quick information access on-line.[6]

The confluence of these variables and the recognition of globally integrated transnational organizations are creating an increased sense of urgency to address the changing demands. One challenge for organizations is to balance being global with operating locally across borders and boundaries. In the intersection of global and local, organizational core values and actions require an approach that recognizes the diversity of the cultures within which they are operating.

Two views on the impact of globalization offer contradictory perspectives on how it is influencing the world. Some believe that as a result of globalization corporations are increasing Western-style consumerism around the world and making common commodities developed in the West—Coca-Cola, McDonalds, Louis Vuitton

(LVMH)—desired worldwide. They propose that this flow from West to East diminishes cultural diversity and produces a homogenization of culture.

Alternatively, others believe that the increase in cross-border transactions increases cultural diversity and spreads pluralism. Cultural attributes take on different forms depending on their contexts, which are referred to as *glocalization*.[7] One example of this can be seen in the branding and advertising efforts of the Hong Kong and Shanghai Banking Corporation (HSBC). Since the beginning of the twenty-first century, it has been possible to land at airports across the globe and be introduced to their "glocal" approach to business as their advertisements asked you to consider the broadened ways in which we can understand differing points of view.

> We at HSBC, the world's local bank, strongly believe in the potential of difference. In a world of increasing sameness, we believe it's important to value different points of view and there should be somewhere everyone can air these views and see the views of others.[8]

People in organizations today have a wide variety of exposure to global diversity, with some being more local and others more international. To respond to this environment, transnational organizations need to create robust learning functions across the globe. The American Society for Training and Development, in its State of the Industry address, claims that globalization is one of the most significant challenges for organizations wanting to address and expand their learning functions to service their locations outside of their home countries.[9] So how do we best lead in this organizational milieu?

## MEETING THE LEARNING NEEDS

This book is intended to address the need to develop cultural sensitivity in the global workplace. The first step is to develop leaders with the ability to relate to others across differences in a way that is respectful of both themselves as well as those with whom they interact. We do not believe that all the responsibility for change rests on the shoulders of the leaders in organizations with diverse workforces. However, we do believe that these leaders have a great influence over the organizational culture and set the tone for how multiculturalism and difference will be addressed within and throughout the organization.

Leadership literature now offers a wealth of information that provides insights, tools, and direction for developing leaders through talent management, coaching, mentoring, learning, and various assessment tools.[10] Our goal is to refocus the literature on developing leaders who will work effectively in an increasingly diverse workforce. By implication, it cannot be taken for granted that the traditional methods we have used in the past will continue to be effective.

This also implies that the definition of leadership success used in the past may need to be redefined. In a global context, members of our organizations will need to become more effective when interacting with others from around the globe or across the hall, particularly when these colleagues represent a variety of cultural orientations and values. We often see that this is not only a matter of proven competence, as leaders deemed competent and successful in one context are not necessarily competent and successful in another. Certain competencies, skills, and approaches to business do not translate well to working with those from others cultures.

Linda A. Hill, Wallace Brett Donham Professor of Business Administration at Harvard Business School,[11] believes that it is useful to reexamine just what an ideal leader is when taking into consideration the degree of change in how organizations need to operate globally. Her research points to the direction she sees leaders will need to take in the next half century to be effective in this ever-changing business milieu. Inspired by Nelson Mandela's autobiography, *Long Walk to Freedom,* and his analogy of a shepherd as a leader, she claims leaders need to "lead from behind" as they create the context for others to successfully take on leadership responsibilities. This image reflects the flexibility needed within an organization or work group, allowing all members to step forward or step back as called upon by recognizing "leadership as collective genius."

We realize that in the creation of more fluid organizations, leaders who are more effective working cross-culturally and cross-border will need to consider ways in which they can appreciate the differences they are being faced with in effectively bringing out the best in those in their workforces. They will need to be consciously aware of the behaviors they are modeling, the work environments they are creating, and the expectations they are setting, as well as how they both reward and hold their staffs, affiliates, and partners accountable.

The burden, or responsibility, does not rest solely on the leader's shoulders. The talented leader needs to be resourceful in engaging others to support this endeavor. These other people will represent diverse voices and perspectives, and, when their views are fully acknowledged, alternative perspectives will be brought into the conversation. This will involve considering the ways in which the global talent pipeline is currently built and further defining what is necessary for leaders from across the world to be successful across cultures and locations.

As alternative ways of conducting business are entertained, creativity will flourish, thereby making the environment fertile for innovation. Nancy Adler, Professor of Organizational Behavior and International Management at the McGill University Faculty of Management in Montreal, Canada,[12] suggests that the leadership challenge we face today is not only reflected in business prosperity, but is also necessary to develop and support society.

## FOUNDATIONAL INFLUENCES

The three disciplines shown in Figure 1.1 inform our thinking and practice.

We believe that effective transnational leaders need to lead in a relational way, taking the whole person into consideration; need to be culturally sensitive and appropriate to the context within which they are communicating; and need to be open to learning and change in the process by fostering and developing their own self-awareness and instilling these values throughout the organization.

Various styles of leadership have been advocated over the years, and these styles have reflected the many ways organizations have been structured to ensure work was accomplished. In the twenty-

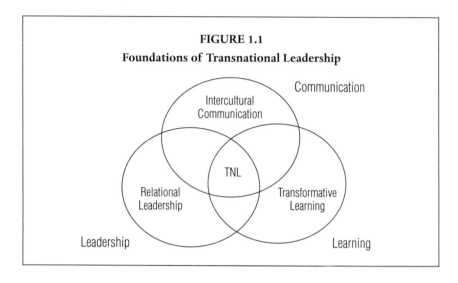

FIGURE 1.1

Foundations of Transnational Leadership

first century the structural forms of organizations are changing again. This is in response to a service economy and the broader range of cultural influences experienced as they become global with a more diverse workforce. In addition, the value the workforce brings to the organization is in the information it possesses and to which it has access. It does not depend entirely on the production of products. The importance of each person in the organization requires a different type of relationship. Relational leadership is more attuned to the differing relationship needs among leader, team members, and stakeholders. Its goal is to create a more inclusive environment based on mutuality and interaction through communication with an ethic of care.[13] Although relational leaders are responsible, accountable, and decisive, they also ensure the commitment and engagement of others by creating a community, establishing a shared compelling vision, fostering a dialogical interaction, being flexible and resilient, guaranteeing time and space for reflection both in and on action, and considering the long-term impact of short-term choices.

Thus, the workforce has become more diverse and the locations of operation are more widespread. As we hear repeatedly that the world is getting smaller and we know from our experience and professional practice that the variety of cultures to which we are exposed continues to grow, the demand for higher levels of cultural sensitivity is increasing. Intercultural communication is an everyday occurrence. The tenets that make for more effective communication across difference need to be consciously incorporated into our psyche, so that we apply them more naturally to facilitate and create smoother conversations.[14] Personal satisfaction and organizational results are directly impacted by poor communication and, when communicating across cultures,[15] the chances for miscommunication are even greater.

When we entertain different ways of viewing a situation, we have an opportunity to understand things in new ways. It is as though we change the color of the light we shine on an object, or we change the angle of the light emphasizing it differently. Changing the color or changing the angle allows us to see the object in a new way. In this process, the object may reveal itself to be different from what we had originally perceived it to be—to be a different size or shape or to have different uses and new meanings. Each new view offers us the opportunity to respond with annoyance or to deepen and broaden our understanding. In this manner, we can say that our view of the object has been transformed. In this way, we can also transform our perspectives about our organizations, the people with whom we work, our products, and even about how we view ourselves.[16] This type of learning, which is transformative, guides us to experience situations in ways we never have before, and to hold these changes so that we never see former objects in exactly the same way again. We have an opportunity to enter into new situations with a new openness, to entertain new possibilities, and to acknowledge that things are not always the way they seem or the way we expect them to be.

The model that follows is founded on the synthesis of relational leadership and intercultural communication. It provides for leadership development through application of the principles of transformative learning. It is a model that provides a view of the paradoxes faced by transnational leaders and provides a framework for determining how leaders are best developed in this context.

# USING PARADOXES

Why paradoxes you might ask? We have found in our practice that leaders often approach situations as problems and then go about seeking solutions. When we identify the solution, we are choosing the answer that we believe best suits our needs at the time. This is a good way to operate when the situations are truly problems. However, in many cases in working across cultures, the situations may not be problems that require solutions but rather paradoxes that need to be managed.

Paradoxes by definition have a contradictory nature and, when this nature is not recognized, a backlash follows. Why? Because the chosen solution may address only one perspective, ignoring others that are equally important. In paradoxical situations, our actions may have unintended consequences that were not originally figured into the equation.

We are suggesting that transnational leaders need to view cross-cultural issues as dilemmas rather than problems, because the issues related to culture and communication can be positioned on continuums with contradictory characteristics. To understand the nature of paradox, take a moment to consider one common dilemma that has defined traditional organizational practices over the years—the challenge of centralization and decentralization (see Figure 1.2).

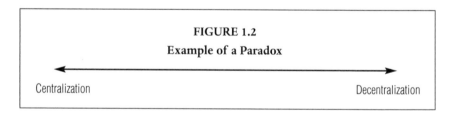

**FIGURE 1.2**

**Example of a Paradox**

Centralization                                    Decentralization

In this example of a paradox, Headquarters (HQ) wants to maintain control over certain practices in the organization by enforcing a policy of centralization of performance management. Therefore, the human resources staff at HQ designs a performance management policy and process that is to be implemented across multiple locations around the world. The policy change is announced and is provided to the locations. As the locations attempt to implement the centralized policy and related processes, they discover that specific points of the policy are not always suitable for their local population. They determine to adapt the policies and gain the approval of the HQ team.

As these offices continue to adapt and modify the policies, it becomes apparent after some time that relevant performance management needs to be managed through a decentralized process. Locations are now left to create policies that align to culture and needs. With time, the organization determines that it needs to put in place a global approach to mobility and decides that decentralized practices create an unworkable solution. So HQ decides to pull in the reins a bit and recentralizes policies for greater ease in mobility. The more HQ centralizes policies, the more the offices complain that these policies are not relevant to their situations. The cycle therefore seesaws from one extreme to the other.

As long as this paradox is framed as a problem that needs to be solved, the pendulum will continue to swing between centralization and decentralization. There will likely never be a satisfactory outcome because it is being framed as an either/or situation. If this were being treated as a paradox, there would be a different framing —and that framing might lead those involved to ask the following question:

> How can we maintain a sense of consistency and fairness throughout the organization, while at the same time ensuring our policies are relevant and useful at each location?

A different type of conversation will ensue in response to this question, as those in both HQ and field locations seek collaboratively to address all the issues affecting this situation; only then will it be possible to be responsive to the needs of both groups.

Research from interculturalists suggests[17] that communication across culture is by its very nature a paradox presenting dilemmas to be considered. The differences learned through first language, cultural traditions, family values, and education create great differences in understanding. What do transnational leaders need to learn about these differences?

American Management Association
www.amanet.org

## THE FIVE PARADOXES

The five paradoxes are listed below and are shown in Figure 1.3.

- Paradox of Knowing: Knowing Self and Honoring Others
- Paradox of Focus: "I"-Centric, "We"-Centric
- Paradox of Communication: Communicating across Difference
- Paradox of Action: Doing and Reflecting
- Paradox of Response: Short Term and Long Term

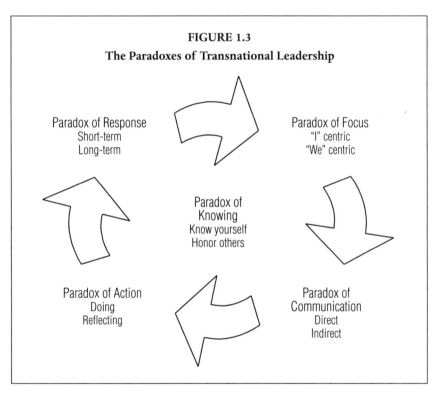

**FIGURE 1.3**

**The Paradoxes of Transnational Leadership**

Paradox of Response
Short-term
Long-term

Paradox of Focus
"I" centric
"We" centric

Paradox of
Knowing
Know yourself
Honor others

Paradox of Action
Doing
Reflecting

Paradox of
Communication
Direct
Indirect

### Paradox of Knowing

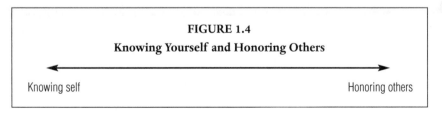

**FIGURE 1.4**

**Knowing Yourself and Honoring Others**

Knowing self                                                    Honoring others

American Management Association
www.amanet.org

This first paradox, "Knowing Yourself and Honoring Others," reflects the tension between awareness of our own needs and those of the other party with whom we are engaged (see Figure 1.4). The key points highlighted in this chapter focus on developing self-awareness, while recognizing our impact on others. "Knowing yourself and honoring others" is a process that involves the following:

- Understanding and honoring the other party and managing the tension of finding the balance between self and others
- Uncovering assumptions we may hold about ourselves and others that influence the effectiveness of our interactions
- Identifying the worldviews (or frames of reference) we hold and from which we operate
- Reflecting on how our worldviews impact our thinking, subsequent actions, and reactions to others

We illustrate this with a short example provided by a participant in one of our recent leadership development programs. Geoffrey, a Tanzanian IT manager, was sent on a 3-year assignment to manage his organization's MIS function in Botswana. Before he went, he didn't consider the implications of moving across countries within the same continent. Rather, he thought about the actual technology issues he would need to face once he arrived.

> I was sent on assignment to Botswana to lead the MIS team through a major system change. I came in acting as I had in my home country of Tanzania. To my surprise, the culture and people were really quite different from Tanzania's and I spent this past year learning what people really meant rather than what I assumed they meant. The rules from my home culture just didn't fit. I didn't fit. . . .

Geoffrey went on an assignment to a different country in Africa within the same organization; he thought that he could apply what had made him successful in Tanzania and be effective. He realized shortly after his arrival that he needed to observe, learn, and rethink how he should interact with the people in this new environment.

He discovered that the rules he used for interpersonal interactions back home were not necessarily relevant in this culturally different workplace.

One way to develop a better understanding of what is transpiring and to elicit a deeper understanding of what is happening in relationship to others is to pose *provocative questions* that stimulate thinking and create opportunities to reflect on the present situation in ways that may differ from what has been the norm. In this case, Geoffrey might consider the following question in the *paradox of knowing:*

> What am I finding challenging in this leadership role and location that I did not experience in previous positions?

Geoffrey realized that his way of leading in Tanzania was not equally effective in Botswana. Rather than force the issue and expect everyone else to adjust to him, the new expatriate in this regional office, he gained an appreciation of the importance of clarifying differences and seeking ways that he could incorporate this new understanding into his team interactions. By becoming more aware, Geoffrey won the respect and admiration of his team members and colleagues. In response to his going the extra mile, others gained cultural flexibility. They recognized who he was because he honored them as he embraced the role of learner.

## Paradox of Focus

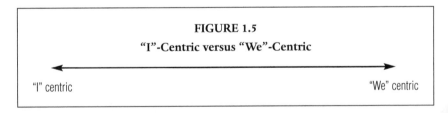

**FIGURE 1.5**
**"I"-Centric versus "We"-Centric**

"I" centric                                                            "We" centric

The *paradox of focus* introduces the contrasts in worldview that exist between those raised in cultures that focus primarily on the needs and interests of the individual (I-centric) and those raised in cultures that place primary emphasis on the collective needs (we-centric) of the group (family, work team, organization, society, etc.) (see Figure 1.5). In this paradox, the tension is in the process of determining whether leadership should

- Be based on the needs of the individual or the group
- Focus on achieving goals or preserving group harmony
- Incorporate both of the above perspectives into a recognition of performance

Whether the focus is on "I" or "we," by selecting the appropriate approach, the leader is better able to consider how to best frame desired outcomes, seek involvement, influence others, and recognize and reward achievement. An example of this difference was shared with us recently by a Swiss banker working in Singapore. Speaking about his new administrative manager, he shared his frustration by noting, "I give her work to do, and later find out it's become a shared project amongst the local admin team."

It is important to develop an awareness of both individual and collective perspectives to consider what is needed in each circumstance. There is a tension that develops in trying to manage this paradox, especially as the individual perspective and the communal perspective require an awareness of expectations in valuing actions and rewarding performance.

Kimi, who was working as a vice-president in an American financial services organization in Japan, related her experiences with the *paradox of focus*. As a young graduate, she was agile and acclimated readily to working with bosses of different cultural orientations, but her learned approach became a liability when she began working with a boss from her own cultural background.

My first three bosses were from the United States. The first one was based in Tokyo, but subsequent promotions found me working virtually for bosses based in Hong Kong and New York. They taught me how to say what I think, and I appreciated that they valued my opinion. All three rated me a star performer! And then when I was promoted to Vice-President I reported to a Japanese manager here in Tokyo, and after 3 months he went to HR wanting to transfer me.

Kimi was obviously surprised at this reaction because she was using her astute and well-honed skills and performing to the best of her abilities. Working from the same location and for the same organization, she believed that she was meeting the expectations of her new boss. Because she was unaware of how her previous reporting experiences had changed her interpersonal orientation from "we" to "me" and because she lacked sensitivity to her current manager's more traditional values and leadership style, she was unaware that her new boss perceived her as ineffective and believed that she was doing something offensive enough to warrant a request for her transfer.

One provocative question for this *paradox of focus* that Kimi considered is the following:

How am I varying my approaches in engaging with my stakeholders?

Kimi considered the factors that made this working relationship similar to and different from her previous ones. Never having worked for a manager from her own country, she needed to consider the importance of differences in cultural orientation. Taking time to consider this question alerted Kimi to differing values that required different actions on her part to be successful in this new reporting relationship.

## Paradox of Communication

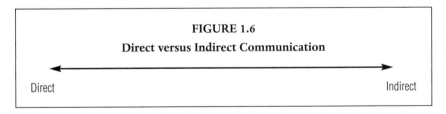

**FIGURE 1.6**
**Direct versus Indirect Communication**

Direct                                                    Indirect

Communication is a necessary and very challenging part of our interpersonal relationships in and out of the workplace (see Figure 1.6).

Many cultural influences affect how we communicate and what we expect from others when they communicate with us. We will be focusing on some of the following key points in this paradox:

- Identifying levels of directness and indirectness that are appropriate in the cultural context
- Recognizing how the understanding of certain words, expressions, and phrases—"yes" . . . "no" . . . "urgent" . . . "work time"— impact subsequent actions and relationship
- Choosing to give information openly or waiting to share it when requested

An illustration of this paradox in action is provided by Petra, a German national working in Hong Kong in Private Banking.

> When I joined the Hong Kong team, I was really challenged. I would ask my direct report to do something and he would say "yes" and then he wouldn't do it. And I would meet with him and make the request again and he would nod and it still wasn't done. This was really a problem that talking directly didn't seem to resolve. I finally sought out cross-cultural training as a means of figuring out how to work with him.

The good news is that Petra was aware that her efforts were not working and sought remedy it before it became a problem.

Petra learned to ask the following provocative question in addressing this *paradox of communication:*

> How can I frame my request so that I understand the intention of others by their responses to it?

Petra took the initiative to address the communication gap between her colleague and she, thereby recognizing that communication is complex and is a shared responsibility. She realized that there was a potential difference between the intent of her communication and the impact it had on her colleague. Knowing this and wanting to be understood, Petra made the appropriate adjustments. In her next meeting with the team member, she reviewed her request with the goal of understanding why he was not taking action. She framed her questions in ways that would allow them to mutually explore the requested work, expectations, and needs. She engaged her colleague in the process as well.

## Paradox of Action

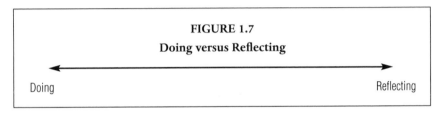

FIGURE 1.7
Doing versus Reflecting

Doing                                                          Reflecting

In the current business milieu, great emphasis is placed on producing results. This puts us into a tailspin of consistent action; we find ourselves always taking action with little if any time to reflect on what it is we are actually doing (see Figure 1.7). In this paradox, we address the following key points:

- Creating balance between doing and reflecting or just "being"
- Recognizing the importance of reflection on leading from an emotionally detached stance
- Reflecting both in action and on action

Reacting emotionally may impair our judgment and lead us down a path we would rather not go. By slowing the pace, we create the opportunity to recognize the influence of our emotional responses and can use the practice of reflection to detach and make better choices. Ideally, leaders need to develop skills to integrate a reflective practice into their behavior. It requires that we reflect on an action after a particular situation takes place to determine what else could have been done; however, it also requires that we reflect in action, that is, in the moment when the event is occurring.

A short scenario illustrating the *paradox of action* was provided by Patrick, the Global Head of Audit for a global technology firm. Joining a virtual global audit team for a firm with significant operations in the United States, Europe, India, and China, and leading from his base in Ireland, Patrick was perplexed by the reactions of some of his team members.

> I always believe you have to know what you have before you start to make changes. Coming in as the third Head of Audit in 2 years, I didn't want to be hasty in setting the vision and direction. I was new to the organization and my first interest was to get to know the enterprise and my team before changing the audit approach. This was my practice in my previous organization, and it had led to my success.
>
> I was surprised to find that the North American staff and management were perplexed at what to do while waiting for my direction. They were quite insistent about the need to move quickly and with a sense of urgency. Clearly they were not in the habit of assessing things carefully and involving stakeholders in the vision.

Patrick entered this situation with previous experiences in mind as to what worked well for him. However, in this situation he received a response from key members of his team and management that differed from his expectations. He learned to ask himself a provocative question, such as the one below, to assess the situation at hand and to determine what the next possible steps might be:

> What is the perceived value of planning versus action? What do I need to understand about the American members of my team and management?

Patrick also experienced some disappointment, as he thought his efforts were in the best interest of staff and management. Still, those based in North America didn't see the initial benefits because his approach was very different from what they expected from a leader. The subsequent confusion provided the opportunity for all involved to consider what they were accustomed to and therefore what they expected to continue, to assess what was different in what they were experiencing, and to acknowledge their emotional reactions to this difference.

## Paradox of Response

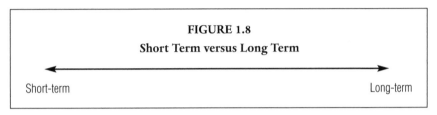

FIGURE 1.8
Short Term versus Long Term

Short-term                                                          Long-term

Our time focus plays a significant role in determining where we focus our attention. It influences the decisions we make and the actions we take (Figure 1.8). The following key points address this paradox:

- Determining whether the emphasis is being placed on past, present, or future
- Developing an understanding of "time culture" and recognizing that not all cultures share the same time orientation
- Identifying both short-term and long-term goals and their advantages, as the purpose and impact of each are different
- Determining socially responsible responses by framing short-term gains in the context of long-term impact and being more conscious of the long-term environmental impact of decisions taken and acted upon today

An illustration describes the frustration that may be a characteristic of the clash that occurs when there is a difference in how time is addressed. Joan was Director of International Human Resources for the New York subsidiary of an Indian Pharmaceutical Company. In my last job I was so frustrated I became physically ill. My boss, the Head of HR, needed to make some decisions on local HR policies. Instead of making a quick and logical response, he would contact Mumbai to confer with the Corporate Head of HR. Every small decision would be delayed for weeks. "So why does HQ in India have to make the decision for a local U.S. company?"

Joan and her boss each had their own reasons as to why decisions should be made either locally or with HQ in Mumbai. They didn't share their diverse views and operated according to the beliefs that each held. In this situation, we offer two provocative questions to help Joan cope with a situation that was creating mental anguish and causing illness:

What did I need to learn about my boss' view of authority and time to make decisions?

What is the short-term impact of a quick local decision and the long-term implications for corporate and local offices?

The first question addresses the different beliefs concerning who holds the authority to make decisions and, therefore, the responsibility that goes along with this. In Joan's view, she saw the issues as related to the U.S. subsidiary only; her boss, who had been born in India and educated in the United States, saw their subsidiary as part of the larger organizational hierarchy and therefore believed that it needed to be directed in collaboration with others in authority. The second question addresses time-based impacts that need to be considered in making any decision.

## USE OF PROVOCATIVE QUESTIONS

The following quotation has been attributed to the great mathematician and physicist, Albert Einstein: *"The significant problems we have cannot be solved at the same level of thinking with which we created them."* As leaders, we need to think differently if we want different results. Provocative questions provide a shift in thinking, allowing us to further understand the context that impacts a particular situation. To engage in understanding any paradox, we need to ask ourselves questions that will guide us to new explanations and alternative responses that will produce more satisfactory results.

## TO CONSIDER

Each of the following five chapters is dedicated to one of the five paradoxes introduced here. Each chapter incorporates a case study that offers one illustration of how that paradox might be experienced. The concepts and provocative questions that are introduced and that are related to each paradox will be explained through the use of the scenario. At the end of each chapter, we offer tools and tips that may help leaders become more effective in their transnational roles. The concluding chapter offers a synthesis of the model and offers one approach for developing transnational leaders.

# 2 | PARADOX OF KNOWING: KNOWING SELF AND HONORING OTHERS

Knowing the Self                        Honoring Others

> *Knowing others is intelligence;*
> *Knowing yourself is true wisdom.*
> *Mastering others is strength;*
> *Mastering yourself is true power.*
>
> —TAO TE CHING[1]

- *Managing the tension of self and others*
- Developing self-awareness
- Respect for difference (intent and impact)
- Identifying world views (frames of reference) and how it impacts thinking and action

## LEADERSHIP, IT'S ABOUT YOU . . .

The core of transnational leadership development is formed on a foundation of self-awareness. Clearly, focusing on self-awareness is not a new concept in leadership development.[2] Each year the *Harvard Business Review* publishes its January issue with the following theme: *"Leadership, it's about you!"* While we agree that self-knowledge and self-awareness are important, our work with global organizations and transnational leaders suggests that leadership is about *you in the context of others*. It is the tension between the leader as self and the leader in relationship to others that becomes the crux of the transnational experience and the framing of this first paradox—the paradox of knowing.

Working within the global milieu requires recognition that the leader's actions may be a reflection of the cultural mores and standards that he or she has explicitly and implicitly learned in his or her family, through early schooling, from the media, and through religious teachings.[3] These early experiences and the national culture that surrounds each person become the programming language for a personal "operating system" as we go through life.[4]

As we move from our home country culture to new cultures or work closely with those from another culture, we are presented with the opportunity to become more consciously aware of how this personal operating system influences our values and beliefs, affects our assumptions, and drives our actions.[5] As we become more self-aware, we also have the opportunity to learn how other people's culture and experiences have shaped them in ways that are both similar and dissimilar from our own. As transnational leaders, it is helpful to understand that in working beyond our home culture or with associates from different cultures, our choice to focus on sameness and difference offers an important perspective that impacts our relationship with others.

Research conducted in the 1960s by Henri Cantril[6] provided evidence that whatever our culture of origin, people share three common needs:

- To exercise freedom of choice
- To assert our own identity
- To achieve personal respect and dignity

Interestingly, while these needs are shared in common, the actions that result in satisfying these needs in your home culture may not have the same impact in another culture. As an example, most Americans experience the "ability to exercise freedom of choice" as the basis for choosing a life partner, a profession, or a lifestyle. The American belief in individual choice frames the people's experiences, and the young adult in this culture will personally select his or her own marriage partner. Traveling to the Gulf countries of the Middle East, Pakistan, India, Bangladesh, and other locales, the "ability to exercise freedom of choice" in choosing a life partner is more likely to be evidenced in the young adult's right to say "yes" or to say "no" to a spouse selected by his or her parents. In these cultures, parents often select a life partner for their son or daughter— someone whose values and background are closely aligned with those of the family. The communal focus that emphasizes ensuring the success and survival of the family unit takes precedence over individual wishes.[7] In both environments, the young adult has "freedom of choice" in the selection of a mate, but the contextual framing changes how this freedom is experienced and evidenced.

Thus, the challenge faced by transnational leaders on a global stage is to understand that while "end needs" may be shared across cultures, exercising free choice may look different in different countries, that how and when we assert ourselves will vary across different cultures, and that what is respectful and offers dignity in one culture may not do so in another. As transnational leaders, it is the tension between self and other, as well as the tension between sameness and difference that will require constant focus and consideration.

## Challenges Faced by José

Consider the challenges faced by José when he was offered the opportunity to move from his company's Atlanta Operations Center to manage an offshore operations subsidiary in Bangalore, India.

---

**FIGURE 2.1**
**Reflection on José and His Actions**

- How are José's culture of origin, his values and beliefs influencing the actions he takes in this story?
- What assumptions did José make that impacted his early actions in Bangalore?
- How was José's impact different than his intent?

---

### Situation between José and Chandra

"The Bangalore Center had been established for a little over 2 years when I arrived. Those first 2 years had been tough, with a lot of miscommunication and misunderstandings between the offshore teams chartered with providing world class customer service and accounting support and the U.S. business units. During those first 2 years, I was based in the Atlanta Operations Center as Vice-President for Customer Service. I had created an effective virtual relationship with the Call Center Division in Bangalore and delivery of telephone responses to our customers were seamless across the two continents. In offering me the Bangalore General Manager role, the organization was asking me to duplicate my success across the Subsidiary.

My decision to accept the offer was a difficult one. As the oldest son and a first-generation American in a Cuban-American family I am very family based. My father had immigrated to the United States in 1960 and he and my mother had recently retired to North Florida from Miami so they would be only a few hours drive away from my family and their grandchildren. I first had to be sure that they would support my accepting an international assignment and being half way around the world before I would actively consider the offer.

My father fully supported it. I then had a conversation with my wife and children to enlist their support for the move. The kids were excited, but Maria, my wife, wasn't initially sure about the move. I suggested to her that being an expatriate wife offered her conveniences she would never have if we stayed in Atlanta. In Bangalore we would have household help and a driver; in addition, and most importantly, my assignment would give her the opportunity to stay home with the children. While Maria wasn't sure she wanted to give up her career, she thought that living in Bangalore would provide a rich experience for all of us; she therefore agreed to try it out for 3 years! With her concurrence I accepted the position.

When we first arrived I was on autopilot. My charter was to ensure that our investment in out-sourcing to India was going to pay off in the savings we had promised shareholders. It was clear that some significant changes were needed to make this a reality.

Upon arriving in Bangalore I had several plans ready for some quick changes that would improve the way business was being conducted between the Atlanta and Bangalore teams. I had met with the Atlanta leadership team before I left and had their commitment to support the changes.

Chandra was a manager and the Head of the Call Center Division in Bangalore. I had previously worked with him virtually. Based on our long-distance success, my first action was to create a new position into which to promote Chandra. He became Vice-President and Deputy Head of the Center the first week I arrived.

My second action was to hold a 'town hall' meeting to introduce myself to our 2,000 employees in the Center. Standing on stage in a large auditorium, I can remember looking across a sea of faces so different looking from the Atlanta workforce, yet charged with the same responsibilities.

At one point in my talk I remember asking the employees if they were aware of the crucial role they played in the organization's success. I stared in wonder as everyone in the audience bobbed their heads 'no.' I was stunned by the response and quietly considered what I needed to say next; I then said, 'I need you to know that customer service is the only differentiator in our industry. What we do here in Bangalore and how we do it is critical, so from this moment on, remember that fact!' In that first speech, my goal was to motivate them by making them realize that they played a very important role in our parent organization's success and that their success would be Bangalore's success.

The employees grew very quiet and I thought that I had gotten their attention and made my point effectively. Later when I debriefed the Town Hall meeting with Chandra, he told me a story about when he studied in England.

He said one of his professors took him aside after the first few weeks of class to ask him why he was disagreeing with everything the professor said. Looking puzzled Chandra said, 'But Sir, I have agreed with you.' It seems that this professor was not aware that in the Indian culture a bob from left to right and right to left means 'Yes, I understand.'

As I listened to this story, I became aware that the Professor and I shared that misunderstanding. Chandra had in that meeting taken on a key role that he played throughout my tenure in Bangalore—he became my cultural interpreter using stories and descriptions of other expatriate's blunders to introduce me to the nuances of difference that I simply didn't see and didn't know.

Then, over the first 4 months of my tenure, I lost 60% of my direct reports as 6 of my 10 department heads left for senior roles with other outsourcing centers in Bangalore. Their loss slowed our progress and challenged my early success. As I reflect on this now in retrospect, it isn't their loss that stands out as much as learning later that it was my first decision to create the Deputy Head role and promote Chandra that first week that precipitated their resignations.

Looking back, I realize that I spent that first year learning what was important to people and what they really meant as opposed to what I assumed they meant. The team in Bangalore was reacting to me based on a way of being in the world that I neither recognized nor appreciated at that time. The rules that I used just didn't fit."

We have seen José's story repeated over and over again in many of the multinational organizations in which we consult with transnational leaders at all levels. Leaders entering into new cultural surroundings or working globally without a conscious awareness of how their own approach to people, to problem solving, to decision making, and to taking action fits within the new cultural context find themselves in a world where the game appears the same, but the rules have changed. Take a moment for reflection and consider (with a bit of imagination) the situation of José (Figure 2.1 on page 25).

## DEVELOPING SELF-AWARENESS

The transnational leader's ability to work effectively across borders is supported by the following:

- Clarity about values that guide actions
- Awareness of social identity
- A deep awareness of the implicit assumptions that drive both actions and responses

## CLARITY ABOUT VALUES
## THAT GUIDE ACTIONS

Leadership research has shown that leaders who are most effective know who they are and what they stand for and act with authenticity. As Kouzes and Posner, authors of the *Leadership Challenge,* have noted, values are "the standards that influence almost every aspect of our lives: our moral judgments, our responses to others, our commitments to personal and organizational goals. . . . values give direction to the hundreds of decisions made at all levels of the organization every day."[8] By consciously acknowledging what he or she stands for and where he or she has emotional investments the transnational leader learns to recognize how beliefs and values influence decisions and actions in the day-to-day world. The transnational leader also needs to develop an awareness that although others may share the same values, they may not act on them in the same way and their actions may not be easily recognized as satisfying the same values.

# AWARENESS OF YOUR SOCIAL IDENTITY

To have this kind of personal clarity the transnational leader must explore his or her earliest personal history, stepping back to view it as if a visitor from another world[9]:

- The context in which he or she was raised: family composition, gender, birth order, economic background, religious orientation, and physical attributes
- Life choices planned and made: educational attainment and goals, military service, career choices, personal relationships, and leisure pursuits
- The recognition of personal attributes: personality traits, aptitudes, strengths, limitations, and motivations

The goal of this exploration is to map your social identity.[10]

Research on social identity indicates that people identify with membership groups with which they share commonalities in background, values, beliefs, and interests.[11] Belonging to these groups allows a person to define his or her identity and foster self-esteem; by being around others who are similar to ourselves we like ourselves more. Conversely, when we are around others who lack our attributes or do not hold membership in the same groups we may discriminate against them because of their differences.[12]

So building an awareness of our social identify is crucial to knowing ourselves and is the basis for consciously honoring others when we move into transnational leadership roles. Figure 2.2 provides one pictorial representation for mapping social identity.

José's story offers the reader a snapshot of his life context, life choices, and personality attributes that may have influenced his values, beliefs, behavior, and actions.[13] José's parents were members of the educated elite who fled from Cuba after Castro's rise to power in 1959. They joined an armada of immigrants who left everything behind to start their lives over again in the United States in the early 1960s. A medical doctor in Cuba, his father was unable to practice in the United States. Through his network of contacts he appren-

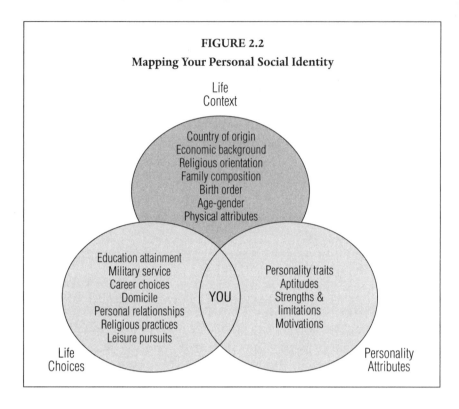

**FIGURE 2.2**

**Mapping Your Personal Social Identity**

ticed himself to a plumber, and by the time José was born he had a thriving plumbing business in Miami. It hadn't been easy, but in his father's view, the economic and political freedom he gained made the challenges and significant life changes worthwhile.

From his earliest memories José recalled his father telling him stories about their life of privilege in Cuba. But rather than focusing on what was lost, his father would focus on his success in recognizing that when things happened that were beyond his control he needed to know what was most important and to act accordingly. From these stories José developed a strong belief in the importance of being resilient in the face of challenge and rapidly adapting to changing circumstances.

As a Cuban-American youth in South Florida, José was bilingual, speaking Spanish in the house and English at school. He moved easily between these two cultural contexts in a bicultural city embracing the strong family values and an element of machismo from his Cuban roots. He learned to appreciate the importance of individuality and taking action with a sense of urgency from the surrounding Anglo-American culture.

So much of who he was as a leader within this organization was based on these prior experiences, his leadership training in the military, the values he took from his family, and his personal style. Figure 2.3 is a graphic representation of José's social identity map.

Stepping into the Bangalore leadership role, José took actions in alignment with his personal beliefs and values, as well as his attributes as a leader, knowing that they provided a compass for his decisions. With a strong sense of responsibility for leading change and personal assurance that he would excel in this new position, he im-

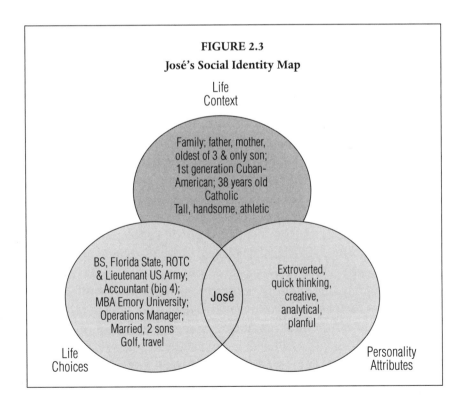

**FIGURE 2.3**
José's Social Identity Map

mediately began to challenge the status quo making quick decisions and taking actions he believed to be in the best interest of the organization. While the intent of his actions was clear to him, the impact of these actions on those in Bangalore was quite different from what he sought to accomplish. To consider this we turn to the role of assumptions in the transnational leader's success.

## A DEEP AWARENESS OF THE IMPLICIT ASSUMPTIONS THAT DRIVE ACTIONS AND RESPONSES

When we consider how we select choices, make decisions, and take actions, it becomes apparent that assumptions are the basis for much of what we do. Assumptions are what we hold to be true; they allow us to take for granted that something is a fact. Our assumptions are generally acquired without conscious awareness, drawn implicitly from the surrounding culture and the sum total of our life experiences. Unchallenged, our assumptions may remain unknown to us, yet they constantly exert a strong influence on our relationships and actions.

When we are in our home culture it is more likely that the assumptions with which we operate will better support our intended outcomes. In our home culture we share a set of common beliefs and values with many of those around us, and past personal experience allows us to determine how people will act and respond. We likely speak a common first language, use similar nonverbal gestures, and recognize the implicit meaning of vocal tone.

As we travel into less familiar places, move into new cultures, or work with others who do not share our common cultural background, we may find that our assumptions and our biases limit our effectiveness. English may be a shared business language but when it is not the common first language, intended meanings and actual meanings may be quite different. There are so many variations of English being spoken around the world that even native speakers have misunderstandings amongst themselves. Now add in the influence of speaking English as a second language and the possibilities for variation of expression and understanding/misunderstanding are multiplied exponentially.[14]

Gestures may have entirely different meanings in different cultures (for example, the "thumbs up" gesture used in America to indicate "great job" is actually an obscene gesture in Australia and Iran). Finally, even our tone of voice may be open to misunderstanding in other cultures. The quiet delivery of a Japanese staff member may be mistaken for lack of confidence or assertiveness or the loud and seemingly harsh tone of an Israeli or an Arab may be mistaken for anger. Working transnationally requires a careful review and a constant checking of our implicit assumptions![15]

Consider, in José's story, the assumptions he was making. Reviewing the story for the explicit and implicit assumptions that José made may provide you with an appreciation for how assumptions may influence our world experience. While we will discuss three of Jose's explicit and implicit assumptions, there are many more to consider in his brief story (Figure 2.4).

---

**FIGURE 2.4**

**José's Assumptions**

In the story José tells he assumed that:

- Maria would enjoy the conveniences of an expatriate assignment even though it meant pausing her career development
- Replicating his working relationship from Atlanta with Chandra in Bangalore would positively influence his success
- A bob of the head from side to side meant "no" in India the same as it did in the U.S.

---

In presenting this new opportunity to his wife José assumed that the ability to be home with the children and the convenience of household help would be strong incentives for Maria to support his acceptance of this expatriate position. Raised in a family in which his own mother did not work, José assumed that this would be Maria's choice. He was surprised when she was reluctant to give up her job and place her career on hold. He had always assumed that she worked as a teacher so they could afford a few more luxuries, and because the job enabled her to spend summers with the children. Talking to her provided him with a new perspective on what she valued. He discovered through the conversation that she valued learning and helping others grow and develop as much as she valued parenting her own children. She believed that being both mother and professional was important. In making the decision to accept the assignment to India, José and Maria agreed to a three-year contract that would allow them to return to the Atlanta area and allow her to return to the District without loss of tenure.

Arriving with a sense of urgency and a need to quickly take charge (after all, those were two of his values), José immediately created a Deputy Head position believing that this would enhance the functioning of the Bangalore Center. He assumed that replicating the working relationship he had when based in Atlanta with Chandra in Bangalore would be important in duplicating their success across the organization. Implicit in that decision were two assumptions:

1. That Chandra was the best person for the role
2. That Chandra's appointment to a Deputy Head role would be readily accepted by the other nine members of the senior leadership team

New to India, José was unaware of the strong hierarchical nature of the local culture. While the Bangalore Center was a subsidiary of an American multinational corporation, its practices in the first two years of operation had generally reflected the local marketplace. It was "acting locally" by adapting its practices to accepted local standards. The six direct report people who resigned from the leadership team were educated in the leading universities in India. They had worked previously in both local and multinational organizations (banks, technology, and accounting firms) and each had over 20 years of management experience.

Unlike many of his colleagues Chandra had been educated in England and began his career for a leading consultancy there. On the

0134112190068

strength of his background he was recruited from England when the new Bangalore Center opened, and although significantly younger and less experienced than his colleagues, joined the Senior Leadership team. There had been some concerns amongst the group then, but over the two years he had done a good job and frequently looked to his colleagues for advice. The group believed that Chandra had recognized his lack of experience and his deference had earned him their respect. Until José's arrival they felt included in leading the Center.

Some of the managers actually felt insulted by having to report to Chandra; after all, they had seniority and they had been mentoring him. Because they believed in deference to authority they did not share these concerns with José. They simply assumed that José did not value them appropriately and as a result sought similar leadership opportunities with other outsourcing centers. While José was outwardly cavalier about their loss, saying "we keep those committed to our success," he found it difficult to source and recruit talent of their caliber in the ever expanding Bangalore operating center market. José at first believed he was weeding out those not dedicated to the Center's success, but after difficulties in recruitment he began to wonder if other dynamics needed to be considered.

And later in his tenure when he reflected back on that first year, he realized that there was so much he hadn't understood about the Indian culture. If he had been more cognizant of the differences relating to power and hierarchy between the U.S. and Indian culture he would have considered the options and perhaps made a different decision.

At the town hall meeting José was unaware that bobbing one's head from side to side meant agreement. To his eyes it resembled an American nonverbal "no" and he assumed it meant the same in Bangalore. He based his message to the employees on his misunderstanding of this key cultural cue, and rather than winning them over, many of his 2,000 employees became wary of the new Center Head. He appeared not to appreciate their knowledge and their contributions.

It is the transnational leader's recognition of the power of assumptions that allows him or her to begin to consider decisions with a kaleidoscopic perspective (Figure 2.5). Starting from his or her own experience and viewing a situation presents the leader with one picture. In the increased complexity of a transnational context, the leader is called upon to turn the lens of the kaleidoscope to see how the same elements may create an entirely different picture of the situation when viewed from anther angle.

---

**FIGURE 2.5**
**By Turning the Lens a Kaleidoscopic Perspective Provides**
**Markedly Different Perspectives Using the Same Elements**

---

With this understanding the transnational leader begins to consider the assumptions that are influencing his or her behavior and to investigate the assumptions that others are using. As the configuration and balance of the elements change, the leader considers the range of interpretations determining his or her actions and responses based on an increased complexity of understanding. The use of a kaleidoscope offers us alternate perspectives of the same elements (situations in an organization): a simple turn of the dial reveals different configurations and patterns through the lens.

Knowing the self requires the leader to create the space and time for reflection; to recognize the assumptions that influence his or her decisions, actions, and behavior; and to gain an appreciation of the subtle and not-so-subtle differences between people from the same and different cultures. While most leadership development and training efforts focus on the knowledge, competencies, and behavior requisite for leadership success, in developing transnational leaders the focus needs to broaden providing the leader with the opportunity to reflect on who he or she is in the context of others, learning how the assumptions that he or she makes may be limiting or altering what is seen, heard, and experienced. As leaders become more aware of the assumptions being made and the values and beliefs that frame the foundation of their thinking, and as they consciously recognize the way culture colors perspective, they become more effective in appreciating others (Figures 2.6 and 2.7).

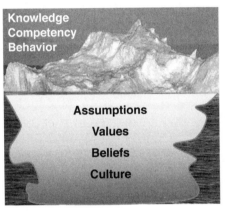

**FIGURE 2.6**

**The Iceberg Model of Self-Awareness**

---

**FIGURE 2.7**

**Attending to Your Own Cultural Influences**

Moving the focus from José to yourself consider:

- How has your culture of origin and your early life experiences influenced your present values, beliefs and assumptions?
- How are your values, beliefs and assumptions evidenced in the way you approach your current role and the people around you?
- How might you need to flex you approach to honor and respect those from other cultures?

# KNOWING YOURSELF AND APPRECIATING THE OTHER: A FIVE-STEP DEVELOPMENT PROCESS

Building an appreciation of intercultural difference follows a five-step process of personal development. When a person first broadens his or her responsibility and assumes a leadership role with a multicultural team or a global division or accepts relocation to a different culture, he or she may do so without being consciously aware of difference. *Differences may exist, but initially do not seem particularly important.* Initially, problem solving, decision-making, and actions continue without being questioned based on the operating system we use, which derives from our culture of origin. That these actions may not be effective in the changing milieu becomes apparent only when we stumble, are faced with opposition, or reflect as a next step to understanding.

As José notes, only after the loss of 60% of his leadership team did he become aware of the unexpected impact (the resignation of six of his direct reports) of his decision to create a new role and his choice to promote Chandra. It is that awareness that led José to the second step of cross-cultural development.

At the second step, *the transnational leader has a growing awareness of subtle conflicts or faces a series of challenging encounters with others that lead him or her to realize that different beliefs and values are guiding actions.* At this step of awareness transnational leaders are likely to continue to assume that their perspective is correct and that the challenge is to influence others who are operating from different sets of values and beliefs to accept "their way." At this step the leader is still not aware of the underlying assumptions that are driving his or her behavior.

When José first realized that his actions led others to leave the team and the organization he sought to understand how communicating his decision differently might have changed the impact of promoting Chandra. Operating from the belief that it is a leader's right and responsibility to make quick decisions in the best interest of the organization, he does not yet accept that differences in values, beliefs, and assumptions—in this situation the value placed on seniority and the view that wisdom is gained with age—may lead to unforeseen results.

The third step involves those who are *ready to begin the exploration of difference.* At this step of awareness, the transnational leader is ready to consider how differences in values, beliefs, and assumptions influence the choices and actions of others. The leader now recognizes that there may be more than one "right" way of perceiving actions and events. At this step in cross-cultural development he or she becomes consciously aware that different "operating systems" lead to different ways of being.

When José views his early actions through the lens of hindsight and with a conscious awareness of the differences between American and Indian cultures, he recognizes that the actions he took in his first week on the job could never be acceptable to the other members of the senior team. Chandra was the youngest member of the team and his promotion to Deputy Head did not acknowledge the respect and dignity that was due to other members of the team. Advancement in the Bangalore context was not based on the meritocracy approach evidenced in Atlanta and at company headquarters in the United States. At this step of cross-cultural understanding José recognized that there is a need to consider different perspectives—his and his direct reports. José needs to act in a manner that recognizes and honors the value that experience and wisdom plays in the hierarchical culture that he has entered. (By understanding this, José learns that he has a role to play in helping his leadership team embrace leadership through meritocracy.)

José may still want to have Chandra support changes across the Bangalore Center; however, with his new understanding of the differences in a cultural context, he will consider a broader range of actions and choices. Honoring the hierarchy, he may create a Project Manager role for Chandra. The questions José must consider at this stage are "how is this leadership situation different from my previous experience and how can I see the world as others do?" After considering these factors, José might then ask the following: "What changes do I need to make to get the results I want?"

At Step 4, the transnational leader *internalizes the acceptance of difference*. Difference becomes the basis for experiencing others. At this step, the transnational leader considers what an authentic connection with each person will require. It is at this stage that the transnational leader shifts his or her worldview trying on new ways of acting in his or her expanded world. Only now is the operating system changed by incorporating new programming that will influence future interactions, leading into the fifth and final stage of cross-cultural development.

In the fifth and final step *the transnational leader fully validates the other.* Viewing others is done empathically, with an acknowledgment of difference and without judgment. At this step, the transnational leader has gained the ability to effectively interact in and out of his or her own culture with true honor and respect for other. The transnational leader is able to do this without much conscious effort because he or she has internalized the different cultural values and is able to act accordingly (Figure 2.8).[16]

While individuals may enter into the five-step process at any level, their growth through the levels is not a function of time but of perspective transformation.[17] The challenge to organizations is to develop learning initiatives that will support and enhance the transnational leader's movement through the five developmental steps.

## THE SELF IN THE CONTEXT
## OF ANOTHER

In addition to self-understanding, to be effective the transnational leader needs to continually consider the people with whom he or she works. By moving out of the standard frame of reference to consider how their understanding may be similar and different, transnational leaders recognize the value of other worldviews. In this

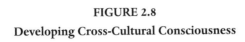

FIGURE 2.8

Developing Cross-Cultural Consciousness

**Step 5:** I fully validate the "other" honoring & respecting our differences and integrate those different ways of action into my own behavior.

**Step 4:** My own world-view is shifting; and I make authentic connection with the "other" based on acceptance of difference.

**Step 3:** I recognize that the "other" has different values, beliefs & assumptions that influence his/her choices & actions; it is my challenge to understand these differences.

**Step 2:** The "other" has beliefs and values different from mine; my job is to "win him/her over to my perspective."

**Step 1:** In regards to the "other," our differences are minimized, and I act consistently across cultures based on my worldview.

process leaders strive to determine the assumptions that are at play in their relationships with each person and to determine how to be true to their own values and beliefs while being appreciative of the values and beliefs of others.

By taking the time to understand others, their worldviews, their values, and their beliefs the transnational leader becomes more open to new ways of seeing and experiencing the world. Successful leaders in a transnational setting lead from a stance of curiosity and discovery, seeking to understand who they are in relation to others and who these others are in relation to them. As a leader moves beyond the borders and boundaries of his or her culture of origin, this awareness of self in the context of the other becomes the basis for success.

# ACTIVITIES TO SUPPORT "KNOWING YOURSELF AND HONORING OTHERS"

## Mapping Your Social Identity

Create a map of your social identity (see Figure 2.9 to assist you with the elements of the map). In a "life context" these are elements that were present in your early life and that are beyond your control. "Life choices" reflect the areas in which you have determined consciously or unconsciously how you will live your life. "Personality attributes" are those elements of yourself that form the basis for your interpersonal interactions.

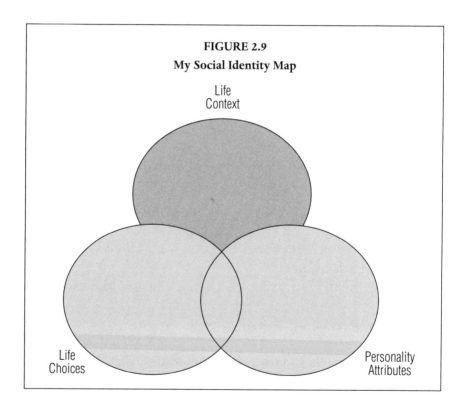

**FIGURE 2.9**

**My Social Identity Map**

## Knowing Yourself: Values Sort Activity[18]

Review the list in Figure 2.10 and identify the 10 values that are most important to you.

---

**FIGURE 2.10**

**Values Chart**

| | | |
|---|---|---|
| Abundance | Commitment | Empathy |
| Acceptance | Compassion | Encouragement |
| Accessibility | Completion | Endurance |
| Accomplishment | Conformity | Energy |
| Accuracy | Connection | Enjoyment |
| Achievement | Consistency | Enthusiasm |
| Acknowledgement | Contribution | Excellence |
| Adaptability | Control | Expediency |
| Affection | Conviction | Experience |
| Agility | Cooperation | Fairness |
| Anticipation | Courage | Family |
| Appreciation | Courtesy | Financial freedom |
| Approachability | Creativity | Firmness |
| Assertiveness | Credibility | Fitness |
| Attentiveness | Daring | Flexibility |
| Availability | Decisiveness | Focus |
| Awareness | Deference | Fortitude |
| Balance | Dependability | Frankness |
| Being the best | Determination | Freedom |
| Belonging | Dignity | Friendliness |
| Boldness | Directness | Frugality |
| Brilliance | Discipline | Fun |
| Calmness | Discovery | Firmness |
| Camaraderie | Diversity | Fitness |
| Capability | Drive | Flexibility |
| Certainty | Dynamism | Focus |
| Challenge | Eagerness | Fortitude |
| Clarity | Economy | Frankness |
| Clear-mindedness | Education | Freedom |
| Cleverness | Effectiveness | Friendliness |
| Comfort | Efficiency | Frugality |

---

**FIGURE 2.10**

(*continued*)

| | | |
|---|---|---|
| Generosity | Loyalty | Professionalism |
| Gratitude | Make a difference | Reasonableness |
| Growth | Mastery | Recognition |
| Happiness | Mellowness | Reflection |
| Harmony | Mindfulness | Reliability |
| Helpfulness | Obedience | Resilience |
| Honesty | Open-mindedness | Resourcefulness |
| Hopefulness | Openness | Sacrifice |
| Humility | Optimism | Self-control |
| Humor | Originality | Selflessness |
| Imagination | Passion | Self-reliance |
| Impact | Peace | Sensitivity |
| Impartiality | Perfection | Significance |
| Inquisitiveness | Persistence | Sincerity |
| Insightfulness | Persuasiveness | Spontaneity |
| Inspiration | Power | Stability |
| Integrity | Practicality | Support |
| Intelligence | Pragmatism | Teamwork |
| Intensity | Preparedness | Thoroughness |
| Intuitiveness | Presence | Timeliness |
| Inventiveness | Privacy | Trustworthiness |
| Keenness | Perfection | Uniqueness |
| Kindness | Professionalism | Unity |
| Knowledge | Reasonableness | Usefulness |
| Leadership | Recognition | Utility |
| Learning | Reflection | Valor |
| Liberty | Reliability | Variety |
| Logic | Resilience | Warmth |
| Love | Resourcefulness | Wittiness |

**FIGURE 2.11**
Values Chart Worksheet

| Ten values most important | My definition of this value |
| --- | --- |
| 1. _____ | _____ |
| 2. _____ | _____ |
| 3. _____ | _____ |
| 4. _____ | _____ |
| 5. _____ | _____ |
| 6. _____ | _____ |
| 7. _____ | _____ |
| 8. _____ | _____ |
| 9. _____ | _____ |
| 10. _____ | _____ |

While you have initially selected your 10 most important values and defined their importance, you are now asked to identify your three priority values and recognize how they knowingly and unknowingly have an impact on your decisions, choices, and the way you live your life (Figure 2.11).

## My Three Priority Life Values

The impact of values is presented in Figure 2.12 and social identity and values are presented in Figure 2.13.

---

**FIGURE 2.12**

**Values and Their Impact on Me**

| Value | How it shapes your life and impacts your decisions and choices |
|---|---|
| 1. _____ | _____ |
| 2. _____ | _____ |
| 3. _____ | _____ |

---

**FIGURE 2.13**

**Reflection on Social Identity and Values**

Individual Reflection: Social Identity and values

- Reflecting on your social identity and values how do they influence your life choices?
- How do they impact upon your relationships with others?
- How do they enhance and limit the effectiveness of your interactions with those from other cultures?
- How are they evident in your behavior as a leader?

# 3 | PARADOX OF FOCUS: "I"-CENTRIC AND "WE"-CENTRIC

| | |
|---|---|
| "I"-centric (individualistic) | "We"-centric (collectivist) |

*Open your arms to change, but don't let go of your values.*

—DALAI LAMA

- "I" or "We"
- Achievement and harmony
- The challenge of recognition

## CONTRASTING CULTURES: "I-CENTRIC AND WE-CENTRIC"

The *paradox of focus* introduces transnational leaders to the contrasts that exist between those raised in cultures that focus primarily on the needs and interests of the individual—I-centric cultures—and those raised in cultures that place primary emphasis on the collective needs of the group (family, work team, organization, society, etc.) —we-centric cultures.

In strong "I-centric" cultures there is minimal group connection and little sharing of responsibility beyond the family and perhaps a very few close friends.[1] Individual focus predominates—my needs, my expectations, my job, my schedule—and people value independence in thought and action, recognition, and reward. In these cultures individuals believe in their own sense of agency and self-determination to make things happen and get results. To be successful in an "I-centric" culture speaking up for yourself is necessary and expected.

Alternatively, in "we-centric" cultures the focus is on group solidarity and responsibility for the well being of each other. People subordinate their personal needs and perspectives to the requirements of the group, valuing belonging to the social network above the need for self-expression. In we-centric cultures the emphasis is on maintaining harmony and showing loyalty; in return for adhering to group expectations individuals receive the security of group membership.

If you were born and raised in the United States, Canada, England, Switzerland, Northern Europe, Germany, or Australia you have been raised within cultural ideologies that foster an "I-centric" view and experience of the world. As a member of an "I-centric" culture you have been raised to be an individual contributor; it is likely that you experience achievement as personal and as a measure of your individual value. Driven to attain personal rather than group goals people in individualistic cultures ensure that their voice is heard, make their points directly, and stipulate what is necessary to ensure success. It is not that people in these cultures don't support group success; it is just that reward structures since birth are targeted to individual performance. Meritocracy is the expressed norm, ensuring that everyone has the opportunity to be recognized for what they do rather than for who they are or who they know. While team success is valued, the primary focus, at work or in sports, is on the performance of individuals, and rewards and recognition target the individual contributor.

Conversely, for people reared in China, Egypt, Bahrain, India, Japan, Korea, the ASEAN countries (Thailand, Laos, Cambodia, Viet Nam, Myanmar, the Philippines, Malaysia, Indonesia, and Brunei), Mexico, Central and South American countries, as well as the majority of African countries the focus and emphasis are on belonging to the group. In we-centric cultures value is placed on the appearance of going-along and the importance of getting-along. To maintain harmony and avoid open conflict communication is indirect and deference is given to those in authority and those with seniority. Group consensus is the preferred style for decisions, and individuals readily put aside personal views to align with the group's direction.

In group-based cultures success and failure are collective events under the direction of the senior member of the group. Individual performance is valued for ensuing the group's success and overt personal recognition. Public recognition and reward are usually offered to the group in its entirety; recognizing team success is done collectively with group dinners serving the purpose of reinforcing the family structure.

Building awareness of the *paradox of focus* is important to the transnational leader. Whether the focus is on "I" or "we," by appropriately selecting the individual or collective approach of either the surrounding culture or a specific member of the team, the leader will be better able to frame desired outcomes, seek involvement, influence others, and recognize and reward achievement.

## GLOBAL PERFORMANCE MANAGEMENT SCENARIO

The paradox of focus has significant implications for working with those from other cultures and doing business transnationally. Consider Patricia and Rosnah's effort to gain buy-in and commitment as they work together to bolster the performance management program of an American multinational organization with a significant and growing presence in the ASEAN region.

---

**Interaction between Patricia and Rosnah**

Patricia was the New York-based Project Manager charged with creating a global performance management system for a Fortune 100, American, multinational corporation. The organization was interested in being able to assess

---

all of its employees consistently around the globe and share data on talent depth and availability across regions. The senior leadership believed that this would greatly facilitate the mobility policy they were encouraging, as well as help to alleviate the challenge they faced when identifying employees for key roles around the world.

The new performance management process would also reinforce a system of merit that ensured fairness to all employees worldwide. The specific goals for this process change were to be able (1) to identify and promote key talents (no matter where in the world they were based) into key positions and (2) to establish "pay-for-performance" as the organization-wide standard for compensation.

To accomplish this, senior management sought to establish a global performance management approach integrated with a pay-for-performance philosophy. The new global process would replace the more than 15 different performance management processes currently in use across the organization. While the U.S. and European offices were already on one shared approach, the offices in China, India, Malaysia, Mexico, Kenya, South Africa, and the UAE had their own individual performance and pay systems in place. A few years ago these locations were relatively small; now each location was employing 2,000–8,000 employees. Clearly it was time to affirm the importance of these locations with a shared performance management approach that would provide consistency in the performance appraisal, succession planning, development, and reward processes worldwide.

Working with a project team drawn from across these locations, Patricia was careful to also directly involve Regional and Country General Managers and Human Resource Heads from these high growth countries in all decisions. Her goal was to ensure that the chosen approaches would have global applicability and impact and that she would have the support of key members of management and those charged with implementing the program during the roll-out.

Rosnah, Head of Human Resources for Southeast Asia Operations (Singapore, Malaysia, Indonesia, and Brunei), a region with over 8,000 employees, was an active member of the design team. At her suggestion Malaysia had been one of the pilot sites for testing the new processes.

Malaysia was selected for the pilot because it was a highly unionized country. Putting the new performance management processes in place required special attention for their leadership teams and line management as well as in-depth explanations to gain the buy-in and support of union leadership.

It had been hard work, and both Patricia and Rosnah were pleased when the union leadership signed off on the global performance appraisal and reward process. The pilot was conducted and management and union alike agreed it was a success. This was important since the new processes were significantly different from those that had been in place previously.

Historically salary increases and bonuses in Malaysia (as well as China and India) were based on position. In the prior year, all clerical associates received 2 months bonus pay and all first-line supervisors received 4 months bonus pay. The number of months paid out was determined annually based on the region's success in meeting established goals. Salary increases were established through negotiations with the unions and were provided to all employees based on their job level.

Under the new system, the performance of individuals at all levels in the company would be personally rated, and salary increases and bonuses would be paid based on the merits of individual performance. The new process would support the identification of key talents in these high growth countries.

When the time for putting the new system fully in place arrived, Rosnah was surprised to discover that the managers in her region had decided to continue to set increases and bonuses based on the historical system. When she met with them she was disappointed to learn that the unions in Malaysia had informally indicated that they would not support the new procedures and the line management had determined that keeping the union as an ally took priority over other new processes.

Rosnah now needed to regain the support of management and their assistance in influencing the union so that the Southern ASEAN Region would be part of the global community. She therefore began to plan her communication strategy.

When Patricia received an e-mail from Rosnah describing the current state of affairs in the Southeast Asia Region she was surprised. She had personally been involved in the meetings with the management team and the unions, and had met with them after the pilot to discuss the success of their trial roll-out. At that time everyone had agreed with the process; she wondered what had changed over the intervening 6 months. Patricia also wondered why she hadn't noticed any signs indicating that the unions and management would not support the new performance management system or why they hadn't come forward with any concerns or second thoughts they may have been having.

Take a moment for reflection and consider Figure 3.1.

---

**FIGURE 3.1**

**Reflection on the Interaction between Patricia and Rosnah**

- How is the "we" based culture evident in the historical way that salary increases and bonuses were determined in the Asean area?
- How is the proposed pay-for-performance process reflective of the values held by an individualistic culture?
- If you were designing a communication strategy to regain the ASEAN leadership, management and Unions what would you do?

---

# THE CONTRADICTIONS IN INDIVIDUALISTIC AND COLLECTIVE CULTURES

In considering the differences between these two cultural orientations —individualistic and collective—it is important to recognize that to be acculturated in one style or the other does not preclude awareness of or the ability to operate from the other's perspective. Our primary acculturation, however, does draw attention to our more typical focus in the world, how we generally enter into situations, hold conversations, make decisions, and take actions.

A person born into the individualistic (I-centric) culture is schooled from infancy to be independent, self-reliant, and self-initiating. Life from an early age is about getting what you need to achieve your personal goals. These people are acculturated to take personal choice as a right, to assert what they need, and to negotiate to achieve their personally desired goals. This is framed in the context of progress and making the world a better place as a result of our own individual efforts.

Walk into a Starbucks in New York City to obtain insight into how individualism is portrayed within the population. People in line not only order their choice of drink from a diverse menu but each personalizes it to his or her specific requirements. The woman ahead of you in line orders a "Venti Mocha"—skim milk, sugar-free chocolate, no whip in a paper cup to stay here"; the gentleman at the next register orders a "plain coffee with 2% milk, *Splenda* (not sugar), and an extra cup." Nobody seems at all surprised by the plethora of special requests; you are, after all, in a society that values "having it your way!"

Conversely, the person born into the collectivist (we-centric) culture is schooled from infancy to place the needs and feelings of the group first. In this interdependent environment, personal needs are minimized and are secondary to the needs of the group. By the age of 2 or 3 years, children have learned to sit unobtrusively and what they require is determined by their parent or parent figure. Individual options are minimized, while ways in which a person can fit into the immediate group are maximized.

Let us visit a Starbuck's in Kuala Lumpur to see how this is expressed. The three young Chinese women in front of you are ordering; one woman orders for the two others and informs the cashier, that "we'll have three coffees with milk and sugar and one slice of cheesecake." The clerk extends the cake providing three forks and they move off to a table. There is no conversation about what to order. The spokesperson has the responsibility to decide the order for the group and the others quietly go along with the choices made; harmony and a sense of belonging take precedent. When the person ordering takes on the responsibility of making a decision for her friends, she tries to make a selection that she believes they will find satisfactory. In the event she orders what wouldn't have been their first choice, they don't complain, but instead show appreciation for the fact that they burdened her with this decision.

These differences are also evident when an office group goes out together for dinner. In London, New York, or Los Angeles a party of six people most likely sits at a rectangular table; each person reviews the menu and personally selects his or her individual choices for appetizers and the main course. The orders are taken from each person at the table and when they are served they proceed to eat only what they have personally chosen. Contrast that scene with an office group of six out for dinner in Beijing, Seoul, Ghana, Kuala Lumpur, or São Paolo. In these countries the party is seated at a round table with a large "Lazy Susan" in the center. One or two of the people at the table—usually those with the highest positions and most seniority—review the menu and order dishes that they believe the others at the table will enjoy. While the person doing the ordering may, on occasion ask others if they have any special requests, this is neither necessary nor a standard part of the ordering process; choices are determined firmly and accepted quietly by all. When the food arrives, members of the group serve themselves from community platters placed on the "Lazy Susan," taking small amounts from each of the dishes, enjoying a shared meal, and most importantly enjoying the common experience. These two experiences become metaphors for the I-centric and we-centric cultural approaches: Western experience framing the uniqueness of each person and the Asian experience framing the importance of the social network.[2]

## "WE-CENTRIC"-BASED
## PERFORMANCE MANAGEMENT

With this framework, consider how the we-centric culture of Southeast Asia was evident in the performance management and compensation approach historically in place in Malaysia.

Everyone in a similar position received the same percentage salary increase and the same bonus. Treating everyone in the same way minimized conflict. As we stated in the scenario the prior year, all clerical associates received 2 months bonus pay and all first-line supervisors received 4 months bonus pay. The number of months paid was determined annually based on the region's success in meeting established goals.

This approach fostered a cooperative approach to work and provided security for all team members. The team as a whole was rewarded for the annual business results, ensuring that everyone's work was considered equally. If individual team members excelled, they did so out of a commitment to team success and loyalty; there was no expectation of individual recognition or reward. And conversely, team members who made an error that negatively impacted business results were not held publicly accountable. Under this style of performance management, the leader of the team took personal responsibility for any failure to meet goals and the team shared equally in its impact. While proponents of "pay for performance" may challenge the collectivist approach suggesting that it lowers motivation and output, it is a standard process that aligns with and supports the collectivist perspective ensuring that harmony is maintained, conflict is minimized, and everyone on the team works for the greater good of the organization.

---

**FIGURE 3.2**

**Behaviors of the Collectivist We-Centric Cultures**

- Groups mimic family dynamics; leaders assume patriarchal roles
- Personal identity and status is drawn from group(s) to which one belongs
- Maintenance of harmony is a priority value and conflict is avoided as a negative force
- Securing the approval of others is a key motivator (individual interests are therefore subordinated)
- Social control is based on fear of "losing face" the possibility of shame and disappointing the group
- Protection is provided in exchange for loyalty and obedience

---

As Figure 3.2 indicates, transnational leaders working with teams from we-centric cultures need to understand the power of the group in motivating performance. The group's success is celebrated, as status comes from the group and not from the individual. The challenge in working with those from we-centric cultures is to understand that because harmony takes precedent communication is not as clear and what is said may not accurately reflect future actions. In conversation with those from we-centric cultures we need to read between the lines and think about what is not being said. We will cover this more thoroughly in Chapter 4 when we discuss communication.

It is important to note that in we-centric cultures each person is responsible for offering "face" to others in the group. "Face" is an important concept that relates to both a person's moral character as well as the social perception of prestige. As such, individual actions that maintain face ensure that trust continues from the social network and that authority related to positional power and influence is honored.

In we-centric cultures interrupting a boss who is speaking or publicly noting an error made by the boss may cause the boss to lose face. Maintaining face may call for team members to quietly accept things with which they do not agree, or even to offer misrepresentations; this is acceptable if it maintains harmony in the group.[3] This is the public side of giving face. There are ways in which subtle, indirect suggestions are made that give face in private, allowing concerns to be aired in a less threatening way.

Intertwined with the concept of face, but separate from it, is the concept of shame. Face relates to the perception that others may think less of you as a result of treatment you receive from someone else. Shame is an internalized feeling that you have let the group down based on your actions.[4] In a we-centric culture the person who is feeling "shamed" has accepted responsibility for his or her choice of actions and the subsequent negative impact of these actions on the group.

We-centric cultures typically have a more ingrained hierarchy, and position and rank are considered when interacting with others. There is protocol involved in gaining access to anyone more than one level above you. You are expected to take problems to your immediate supervisor and not to anyone beyond. New opportunities typically are offered to the most senior person, not necessarily to the person best suited for the job.

Although there is a shared sense of responsibility within the group, it is the person with the highest rank that accepts responsibility for all problems and personally absorbs the shame and humiliation for the group. This is why when there are scandals in Japan it is common practice to see the heads of corporations or government officials resign; they accept blame because they should have better directed the group. There is a belief that when an individual accepts the burden of responsibility for any wrong-doing it negates the responsibility of a corporation or government and restores credibility and trust.

Figure 3.3 lists the business implications of a we-centric focus for a transnational leader.

---

FIGURE 3.3

Business Implications of a We-Centric Focus

- Relationships are valued and take precedence over task accomplishment
- Public agreement is given to avoid conflict (agreement does not necessarily align with subsequent action)
- Public anger toward an employee's actions is likely to result in loss of face for both parties and possibly shame for the employee who's being publicly confronted
- Group recognition, reward and celebrations reinforce and foster sense of family

---

In the collectivist focus, where the social network predominates, the transnational leader needs to learn that relationships take priority over task accomplishment. The focus is on building a sense of mutual commitment. The need to involve "the family" decreases the tendency to take immediate action, with the focus more on achieving consensus. In the collectivist setting, ensuring that you have buy-in is less about achieving agreement and more about meeting with people one-on-one prior to a meeting or the launch of a new concept, product, or policy to obtain their input and feedback. If you value the expression of differences of opinion then you will need to create personal conversations in which others may take the opportunity to disagree with your view in private. Remember, as the leader, your group members will be seeking to maintain face (yours and theirs) and public agreements may be social representations of the appropriate response, but not necessarily agreement.

This is a very familiar experience for many and often fools people into thinking that there is smooth sailing ahead. They are then surprised and confused when no action has taken place after what they thought was obvious agreement. When this happens repeatedly it leads to frustration and may damage relationships as distrust grows on both sides. The person believing there was agreement now distrusts the person seeking to save face and finds it difficult to believe anything they say. The person trying to save face now distrusts the person thinking there was agreement for their naiveté and lack of awareness. They also lose confidence in the ability of this "insensitive" person to effectively lead them.

Finally, if you are from an I-centric world, and find yourself in a we-centric business setting, you will need to rethink recognition and reward. Team meetings are places to recognize the efforts of the group. If someone is not performing then your best action is to shame them privately into the recognition that they are letting the group down by their actions. You will need to manage their sense of shame carefully; if they believe that others have lost trust in them they may conclude that they need to resign. What you don't want to do in this situation is give public credit to an individual. This may embarrass them, the group may be insulted, and it may create disharmony and dysfunction in the group rather than act as a motivator as it would in an individual setting.

## "I-CENTRIC"-BASED
## PERFORMANCE MANAGEMENT

Performance management in "I-centric" cultures has its roots in the early industrialization of the United States and France. Drawing from the work of two influential contributors to modern concepts of management—Frederick Taylor and Henri Fayol—the individualized performance management concepts we use today were developed between 1880 and the 1920s by industrial engineers for the steel industries.[5] From these early origins the foundation of performance management has focused on recognizing and rewarding efficient individual performance, believing this will motivate all to continue trying harder and improving overall performance.

The performance management process begins with objective setting: each member of the team sets personal goals that align with group strategy, each person on the team is individually accountable for meeting agreed expectations, an annual formal appraisal is conducted for each person in the work group, and salary increases and annual bonuses are established to recognize the value of the individual performer. While technically everyone on the team can meet or exceed their goals, the process is predicated on encouraging people to exceed expectations and outperform each another.[6]

To drive individual performances organizations frequently use the "bell curve," which allows only the top 5% of the employees to receive the highest rating. Proponents of the collectivist approach point out that this process rewards individuals who meet their goals even at the risk of negatively impacting team results. They further note that the process fosters a competitive spirit and limits the ability of the team to work together effectively.

The global process created by Patricia's project team drew heavily on the individualistic approach to performance management. For the first time under the new system, the performance of individuals at all levels in the company would be personally rated, and salary increases and bonuses would be paid based on the merits of individual performance. The new process supported the identification of key talents in high growth countries and reflected the process currently in place in the United States and Europe where over 30,000 employees of the corporation were based. The project was as much about bringing the developing countries in alignment with Headquarters as it was about creating a new approach to performance management. Because of this Patricia had purposely sought the involvement of the Regional and Country General Managers and Human Resource Heads from the high growth locations to ensure that the new processes would meet the needs of local staff.

Like many multinational organizations over the past decade, her company had made an effort to honor the diversity of their workforce ensuring that locally hired employees were in leadership roles. Yet what differentiated the General Managers and HR Heads from the middle and front line management and clearly the union leadership is that almost all had been educated in the United States, Australia, or the United Kingdom. And all of the General Managers had lived and worked in the United States before returning to their home cultures. Having had the experience of living, studying, and in some cases working in more I-centric cultures, no one on the team took issue with or expressed concern that the proposed processes were by their nature individualistic. Their schooling and early work experiences enabled them to consider the more individualistically oriented performance management system as acceptable.

Figure 3.4 details some of the classic behaviors of individualized "I-centric" cultures.

---

**FIGURE 3.4**

**Behaviors of Individualist I-Centric Cultures**

- Individual achievement and power are valued
- People look after themselves (and at most their nuclear family),
- Honesty is valued, sharing one's view is expected and conflict is an inevitability
- Public recognition is appreciated, and individual blame for mistakes accepted
- Social control is based on fear of losing "self-respect"
- Succes or failure is based on individual actions

---

As Figure 3.4 indicates, I-centric cultures focus interaction on the individual. In these cultures it is expected that "people look after themselves" and others are on their own. Success and failure are individual accomplishments to be acknowledged and celebrated publicly with people being singled out for actions that support a successful outcome. Because individual achievement is valued it is sometimes more difficult for people in these cultures to ask for help.

In an I-centric culture it is desirable to speak openly and honestly regardless of a person's position. Debate is a common form of conversation where people compete to have their point of view heard and disagreement and conflict are accepted as a logical part of the process. Open communication is believed to be better because it allows the best ideas to be shared and selected. Disagreement plays a significant role in I-centric cultures; it is seen as a process that helps improve good ideas and makes it possible to discard ideas with evident shortcomings.

Whereas in we-centric cultures social control is managed through "face" and "shame" in me-centric cultures social control is gained through guilt. The Merriam Webster on-line dictionary defines guilt as "feelings of culpability especially for imagined offenses or from a sense of inadequacy," noting that it results in a "sense of self-reproach." So while "shame" is based on letting others in our in-group down, guilt is based on an individual believing that his or her actions or behavior did not measure up to a perceived standard, resulting in negative feelings about oneself.

---

**FIGURE 3.5**

**Business Implications of I-Centric Focus**

- Task accomplishment takes precedence over relationships
- Public disagreement is commonplace and conflict inevitable
- Providing an honest response that expresses one's opinion in group settings is expected
- A person can accomplish anything through hard work
- Recognition, reward and celebrations reinforce individual achievement

---

In the individualistic focus, where personal achievement and individual power predominate, the transnational leader needs to learn that task accomplishment is perceived as being completed most efficiently through individual efforts (Figure 3.5). When work needs to be done, people will say and do what they believe is necessary at the time to accomplish their goals. There is little concern for creating a sense of teamwork because in the spirit of efficiency, building relationships and consensus and coordinating efforts are too time consuming. The main focus is on reaching goals. Time is of the essence. A common assumption is that people from individualistic cultural orientations are not people-focused and do not have the ability to work in partnership with others. The reality is that teamwork is just done differently in a more collectively oriented environment, where time is a factor, but not the driver of actions. We discuss the influence of time focus at greater length in the Paradox of Response (Chapter 6).

In I-centric work, people say what they think; they may challenge the ideas of their boss publicly and place a value on the merits of conflict and disagreement. In these cultures it is believed that the expression of different opinions will lead to improved outcomes. A transnational leader in we-centric cultures working with a person raised in an individualistic culture will have to inform the team member of the standards and expectations accepted in their new environment. While others may allow them to voice their opinion at will, they will need to learn the nuances of "me" versus "we."

# ACTIVITIES TO SUPPORT "I-CENTRIC AND WE-CENTRIC" ORIENTATIONS

## Assessing the "Paradox of Focus"

Assess your current work environment considering each of these characteristics. For each characteristic first define the criteria and provide the rating level—High, Medium, or Low—for the situation on which you are focusing (Figure 3.6).

**FIGURE 3.6**

**Assessing the Paradox of Focus**

| Characteristic | Criteria—define for each characteristic | High | Medium | Low |
|---|---|---|---|---|
| Independence in working style. | Working Style (define) | | | |
| Interdependence in working style. | Working Style | | | |
| Open communication in group. | Communication | | | |
| Open disagreement or conflict. | Conflict | | | |
| Time and efficiency are a priority | Time | | | |
| Care taken to not offend any group member | Interpersonal Dynamics | | | |
| Expedient decisions reached | Decision-making | | | |
| Assuring consensus for decisions. | Decision-making | | | |
| Praise given to individual accomplishments. | Recognition | | | |
| Praise given to group accomplishments | Recognition | | | |

Based on the ratings you have given to these measures, think about specific strategic actions you can take to foster better working relationships (Figure 3.7).

**FIGURE 3.7**

**Planning Your Strategy for the Paradox of Focus**

| Criteria | Strategic action steps: |
|---|---|
| Working style | _____ |
|  | _____ |
| Communication | _____ |
|  | _____ |
| Conflict management | _____ |
|  | _____ |
| Interpersonal dynamics | _____ |
|  | _____ |
| Decision making | _____ |
|  | _____ |
| Reward or recognition | _____ |
|  | _____ |

# 4 | PARADOX OF COMMUNICATION: COMMUNICATING ACROSS DIFFERENCE

Direct                                              Indirect

*The most important thing in communication is to hear what isn't being said.*

—PETER DRUCKER[1]

Although there are many considerations in communication, we will focus on three in this chapter. In considering how to communicate effectively across difference our attention is drawn to three points:

- First to the interaction between the speakers (direct–indirect)
- Then to the shared and disparate meaning of words, expressions, and phrases (words–expressions)
- And finally to the style of delivering the message (linear–circular)

## COMMUNICATION IS THE CHALLENGE FOR TRANSNATIONAL LEADERS

As a transnational leader you are either working or living in a culture different from your own or working with others of different cultural orientations, or perhaps a combination of the above. While there is usually a shared business language in the workplace, under-

American Management Association
www.amanet.org

standing what is being said and the true intention of the message is not always as easy as it may first appear.

What you say and how you say it may not be heard or experienced by another person in the way you intended. As communication is a reciprocal process, you also may not be experiencing what others say to you in the way they intended.

## BERNARD AND WAI TING: THE CHALLENGE OF BEING TRANSNATIONAL

A short case will illustrate this phenomenon.

---

### Conversation between Bernard and Wai Ting

Bernard asked Wai Ting, one of the staff members on his team, to create a report that he urgently needed for an upcoming meeting with his boss. Wai Ting listened to the request, and said "Yes." Hearing the "yes" Bernard assumed the report would be on his desk the next day.

After three days, Bernard had not received the report. He approached Wai Ting asking for the report. Wai Ting responded, "Yes, I am working on it." She then began to tell Bernard about the difficulty she was having with a different project.

Bernard was frustrated that the report wasn't ready and further baffled by Wai Ting's reply concerning another unrelated project. He knew he had been clear in his request. As a result of his frustration he cut her off and said to her, "Which part of the phrase 'The report is urgent.' didn't you understand?'" Wai Ting became silent and looked down.

---

What had transpired between Bernard and Wai Ting? To be able to answer this question requires you to "experience the world as Bernard and Wai Ting" do.

Bernard had come to Singapore five months before as a mid-level manager for a Global Fortune 50 Technology Company. He was finding the transition to life in Singapore trouble-free. It was a lot like life in the United States, with Friday nights out with his staff, golf on Saturday, and access to most of the conveniences of home. While his staff was multicultural—Singaporeans of Chinese, Malaysian, and Indian background—English was the common language shared by all. Taking on the management of this multicultural team and working effectively with each team member was from Bernard's perspective relatively easy.

Before coming to Singapore, Bernard had been a manager in the New York City office of the same organization. Through his accomplishments he was identified as "high potential" in the corporate talent management process. The organization was lacking depth in its talent pipeline and managers of Bernard's caliber were important for the future as the organization grew globally. This was Bernard's first overseas assignment and with future growth forecast primarily in the markets of Asia and the Indian subcontinent, it was important both to the corporation and to Bernard personally that he succeed.

Upon arrival in Singapore, Bernard continued to lead and manage as he had in his former role. As an American, he was focused on achieving outcomes, used to saying specifically what he needed, hearing "yes" as full commitment to action, and using the word "urgently" to indicate immediately. In his mind it was all very straightforward.

While Bernard assumed that Wai Ting was Singaporean (after all she looked like others on the team), she was not. Wai Ting was recruited from the Masters in Business program three years ago from Tsinghua University—the MIT of China. Wai Ting's transition to the company and Singapore was also relatively uncomplicated as she moved to a small island nation with two million people where 79% of the population was Chinese. While sharing a common historical Chinese heritage with many of her colleagues, because Wai Ting had been raised on the Chinese Mainland and born after the Cultural Revolution, her style of interaction and communication was quite different from her Singaporean Chinese colleagues; who were second generation Singaporeans. Wai Ting was raised in a culture in which the needs of the group took precedence over one's personal needs, where deference to authority was embedded, and where communication was offered in an indirect manner that significantly relied on paying attention to what was unexpressed as well as the nonverbal communication.

Like Bernard, Wai Ting had been very successful since joining the organization. After only 18 months with the company she too was identified as a "high potential" in the talent management process and had been promoted to a senior consulting role by her prior boss. Talent like that shown by Wai Ting was particularly important to the organization as the company saw the China market as a significant area of growth for the coming decades. Young professionals like Wai Ting who had worked off-shore and understood the organization's culture of innovation and passion for excellence would assume key leadership roles as the China market expanded. In the company's succession planning process, Wai Ting was targeted for her next promotion within the year. From an organizational perspective she was the kind of talent they required to secure their future growth—bright, capable, and on the fast track!

Since Bernard arrived as her new manager, Wai Ting continued to deliver a strong performance, but she wasn't as comfortable on the job as she had been. Bernard seemed to say things with an unnerving directness; and he didn't seem to take the time to listen to what she had to say. He would frequently cut her off when she was speaking and say "so what's your point?" when she was clearly explaining her point; if he would simply take the time to listen. While Wai Ting did not share these thoughts with anyone, she thought Bernard was impatient and quite rude in the way he spoke. She felt silenced (Figure 4.1).

---

**FIGURE 4.1**

**Reflecting on the Conversation between Bernard and Wai Ting**

Take a moment for reflection and consider . . .

- Who is/are the transnational leader(s) in this case?
- What cultural influences are effecting the communication between Bernard and Wai Ting?
- What are the career and interpersonal risks for Bernard and Wai Ting in this situation?
- What are the organizational risks present in this situation?

---

# WHO IS (ARE) THE TRANSNATIONAL LEADER(S) IN THIS CASE

In today's global organizations, many members of the same team may be "transnational leaders." While the primary image of the transnational leader may be the manager or leader working outside his or her home culture, we encourage you to expand on that definition and include professional team members working outside their home culture, as well as managers leading teams with membership from multiple cultures.

With this perspective, Bernard and Wai Ting are both transnational leaders in this organization. Each has relocated to Singapore to work, coming from home cultures in which they have been high achievers. Bernard has proven himself as a manager, leading a high performing team in New York, and is at the beginning of his global career, and Wai Ting, a top MBA graduate, is on the fast track and slated for a significant leadership role as the China market matures. Based on their tenure in the organization both are ranked in the top 10% of all employees and are identified as "high potentials" through the talent management process. American and Mainland Chinese raised, neither has had previous experience in working with someone from this other culture. Working transnationally without conscious recognition of their differences they stand at a professional crossroads.

# WHAT CULTURAL INFLUENCES ARE IMPACTING THE RELATIONSHIP BETWEEN BERNARD AND WAI TING?

As you reflect on the background of Bernard and Wai Ting, what stands out for you? If you are from the United States like Bernard you might find it easy to relate to how he acts. If you haven't worked with someone from China before you may be confounded by Wai Ting's actions. Perhaps as you read their story, you are thinking that it seems so straightforward: when your boss asks you to do something "urgently" you either get it done the same day (or the latest the next day) or explain to him why it isn't possible.

This was Bernard's belief based on how he had been acculturated within the American society. Born on the East Coast of the United States, he was a quick thinker and a fast worker. Like most Americans "time was of the essence" and getting things done with quality and on schedule was the basis of his success. He was acculturated in a society that values speaking directly and to the point and in which you stand up for your individual rights and present ideas without hesitation. In Bernard's experience and worldview, if a subordinate disagreed or was unable to directly comply with a request they should say so. If this created a short-term conflict it was better than avoiding or not discussing issues early on and waiting until they escalated into something major.

Yet, if you grew up in China, you would understand that saying "yes" to a request from your boss supports the three primary functions of communication in the Chinese culture: to preserve harmony, to reinforce role and status differences, and to maintain existing relationships. Through this lens, perhaps it becomes a bit clearer that Wai Ting's initial "yes" to Bernard's request did not necessarily have the same meaning as Bernard attributed to it. Given his role and the status difference—he was her boss—saying "no" was not an option for Wai Ting; in wanting to preserve harmony saying "yes" was the best alternative. From a Chinese perspective establishing and growing relationships are the basis for success in life and work, and taking time to develop relationships is more important and has more of an impact on your career even than doing good work.[2]

Based on her cultural context, when Wai Ting responded to Bernard's query about the report by telling him about other problems that required her attention and were taking her time, she expected him to understand the meaning behind her words. In her own culture a manager would recognize this kind of explanation as an indirect way of initiating a conversation in which each could explain and explore issues and needs safely. Wai Ting was quite surprised when Bernard cut her off and asked "what part of urgent don't you understand?" Not knowing how to react to his (seeming) attack and searching to reestablish harmony she simply looked away.

## WHAT ARE THE CAREER AND INTERPERSONAL RISKS FOR BERNARD AND WAI TING IN THIS SITUATION?

Clearly the differences in their cultural programming have the potential to derail one or both of these corporate talents. Continuing in this manner may impact the careers of both Bernard and Wai Ting.

- If the miscommunication continues with Bernard it is likely that Wai Ting's actions may be identified as a performance problem that needs management. Bernard may conclude that Wai Ting is simply not as talented as her previous boss indicated. This is a classic story that happens all the time; when the boss changes, a person is measured against different standards and may not live up to his or her prior reputation. In this situation, even though it may be Bernard's cultural blindspot that impacts this shift in assessment, Wai Ting may suffer all the same.
- Bernard's boss, a Singaporean who participated in the identification of Wai Ting as key talent, may be expecting Bernard to know how to effectively manage staff members from other cultures. Bernard may be judged to be unable to effectively manage a global team and may be seen as a poor fit for a continuing expatriate assignment, which may be career limiting in this organization.
- Responding to Bernard's attacks (her perception), Wai Ting may withdraw and become demoralized and her motivation to perform may be impacted. In her frustration at not being heard Wai Ting may begin listening to the search recruiters who are calling her up and begin looking for career opportunities outside her present organization.
- The level of trust between Bernard and Wai Ting may be eroded based on how each is interpreting the others' actions through their diverse cultural filters. As trust decreases the stress in their

working relationship increases and the emotional well being of one or both may be impacted.[3]

So depending on their future interactions and decisions both "high potentials" are at risk of career derailment based on their interpersonal relationship and cultural misunderstandings.

## WHAT ARE THE ORGANIZATIONAL RISKS?

This organization is presently at risk of losing two talented leaders with the potential for present and future organizational success. Let us assume in this case that both Bernard and Wai Ting are indeed "high potentials," and that it is their limited recognition of intercultural differences that creates their communication challenges and stands in the way of them working together effectively at present and in the future. From an organizational perspective, the focus needs to shift from managing a problem employee or having a difficult conversation to identifying the skills, capabilities, and tools that will best support each person in becoming a more effective transnational leader. Bernard's boss and the organization are at a critical moment for intervention.

## WHAT DO YOU NEED TO UNDERSTAND ABOUT INTERCULTURAL COMMUNICATION?

Approximately 60 years ago the field of intercultural communication was formally established. One of the fundamental principles that guide thinking and knowledge about intercultural communication is that "the core of culture is communication."[4] While a simple concept, there is incredible power in understanding that it is language that determines what we see, what we know, and how we relate to others. Language provides the filter for our experiences.

How we communicate with others is based on our "mental software" programmed through first language, cultural traditions, and our early family experiences.[5] Our cultural conditioning provides us with a particular lens or frame of reference from which we act and understand the actions of others. As long as we remain within the boundaries set by our birth culture, and the culture within which we spent our formative years, we may not even be aware that how we view the world and act in it may be radically different from others raised in different cultures.

For example, through the lens of your country of origin consider the "correct way of setting the table for dinner." In the United States etiquette calls for the fork to be placed to the left of the plate and the knife followed by the spoon is to the right. In Thailand a large spoon and a dinner fork are placed to the right of the plate. The fork is used only to move the food on your plate onto the spoon; the spoon is the utensil for bringing food to your mouth. In China chopsticks are placed vertically to the right of the bowl, while in Japan they are placed horizontally between the person and the bowl and rest on a chopstick holder. There are separate chopsticks used to transfer food from central serving dishes in bite-size portions to your bowl. In India, Saudi Arabia, and numerous other countries, no utensils are provided, as they are not necessary. However, touching food is done only with the right hand, never the left, for sanitary reasons.

By moving beyond our home borders we come to learn that there is in fact no correct way to set a table, just different approaches related to specific cultures and traditions. This example serves as a metaphor for communicating effectively as a transnational leader: there is no one best way to communicate. Being effective requires that we learn the nuances of the other person's culture and have the flexibility to work with that person's style and, conversely, that we need to support them in being able to do the same.

While English is the common business language for multinational corporations in many places in the world, it is not necessarily used and understood in a universal way. Even when an American and someone from Britain are having a conversation the two may use entirely different words to describe the same objects without shared comprehension—elevator versus lift; trunk versus boot; restroom versus water closet; toilet versus loo. Unless you have learned the idiosyncrasies of English in different settings there is the potential for communication failure.

It is the nuances of meaning between cultures that frequently lead to miscommunication and misunderstanding. As we consider the paradox of communicating across cultures it is important to first recognize that there are differences between cultures that cause meaning to be implicitly understood through contextual cues—high context cultures, in comparison to cultures that have a stronger reliance on words themselves to ensure common understanding—low context cultures. In *high context* cultures (e.g., China, Northeast Asia, Southeast Asia, the Indian subcontinent, Indonesia) communication is highly implicit and meaning is made by taking clues from the setting, from what has come before, by attending to nonverbal cues, and by considering what isn't overtly stated as much as what is. For example, in a one-to-one meeting to discuss a promotional opportunity with a team member who has been offered a new job that requires relocation, the high context manager might simply smile, nod affirmatively, and say "You hold the trump card!" leaving it to the employee to interpret the meaning of this statement on his or her own. No further words are exchanged. The employee in the high context culture considers his or her status in the organization, his or her relationship with the boss, and the nonverbal indications made during the conversation and recognizes that even if he or she does not accept this relocation offer, the organization will continue to value him or her as an employee.

In *low context cultures* (Australia, Canada, the United States, and Western Europe) the focus is on an explicit use of words to fully explain and ensure agreement. That same conversation with the employee in a low context culture would more likely sound like this: "You hold the trump card, there is no one else with your skill set, and the company needs you. So whether you accept the relocation or not there is a job for you and you will remain a valued high potential contributor." When low context and high context groups come together in a shared setting the different sets of rules, protocol, and expectations of what gets said, not said, clarified verbally, or expected to be understood without further elaboration becomes the challenge of

communicating across difference. In low context cultures communication tends to be direct, expressive, and linear; in high context cultures communication tends to be indirect, restrained, and circular.

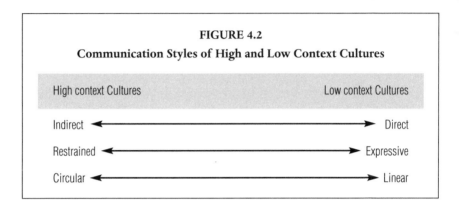

**FIGURE 4.2**

**Communication Styles of High and Low Context Cultures**

High context Cultures                                    Low context Cultures

Indirect ◄─────────────────────────────► Direct

Restrained ◄─────────────────────────────► Expressive

Circular ◄─────────────────────────────► Linear

Figure 4.2 shows the three contextual dilemmas of communication—direct versus indirect, expressive versus restrained, and linear
versus circular—aligned to high and low context cultures. As American and Chinese cultures tend to represent the opposite poles of
these continuums it is easiest to articulate the differences of these
dilemmas through examples contrasting their behavior. Why they
are placed in opposition to one another is based on foundational values for each culture—for the Chinese the key value is relationship
and for the American the key value is achievement—and it is these
framing values that provide the foundation for speaking, listening,
and understanding.

## THE DILEMMA OF COMMUNICATING WITH
## WORDS: DIRECT AND INDIRECT

A key purpose of communication is to create shared meaning between the communication partners. Within a culture this is achieved
in a variety of ways with assorted techniques and accepted roles, and
each role has ascribed responsibilities and expectations. From a cultural context, the speaker and listener are expected to behave in cer-

tain ways. At the risk of over generalizing and realizing there are variations on a continuum within any culture, Americans value task accomplishment and are generally focused on efficiency and effectiveness. Hence, in communication, comparatively speaking, Americans are exceptionally direct and to the point using specific words to explain their thinking and state their needs. Words for an American are literal and form the basis of communication. Within American culture it is the speaker's responsibility to communicate in a way that the listener will understand and the speaker's responsibility to explicitly check for understanding. Assumptions are to be surfaced and explored.

In contrast, the Chinese place importance on relationships as the vehicle through which meaning is made, with the goal of maintaining harmony through public consideration for the other person. The Chinese are indirect, believing that words are not sufficient to express meaning and that the listener will best understand thinking and needs through inference and reflection because there is an assumption that they share a common context as reference. In the Chinese pattern communication success is more the responsibility of the listener, as meaning lies as much in the unsaid as the said. Acting on assumptions is encouraged.

Both communication approaches offer value. Being indirect ensures the continuance of outward harmony and the maintenance of the relationship; being direct ensures that tasks are accomplished.

These two cultures may use the same words with entirely different meanings. In a staff meeting when the team is asked, *"what do you think about this project,"* by an American colleague, they are usually being asked for feedback and input. There is a belief that a better quality project will result from others providing constructive feedback. Being asked, *"what do you think about this project"* by a Chinese colleague is contextual. It may be that the colleague wants others on the team to be aware of the project's existence or hopes that others will actively support the project; however, it is likely that he or she is not seeking feedback. The indirect query and response minimize the risk to a working relationship or the potential for a loss of face by the speaker.

## THE DILEMMA OF COMMUNICATING FEELINGS:
## EXPRESSIVE AND RESTRAINED

Americans are taught to speak out assertively as a sign of confidence. The American is encouraged to say *"yes"* or *"no,"* disagree publicly, and to do so with minimal regard for positional and role authority because the disagreement is being framed as disagreeing with the idea and not the person. Hence, in team meetings you will frequently find that these team members are the first to speak up, freely disagreeing with colleagues or even the boss, challenging the other's thinking and actions, and offering their own views as a constructive contribution toward shaping the end result. Criticism is not to be taken as personal, intended, or implied.

From this basis, when Americans move to Chinese cultures, they will frequently continue to use the team meeting as a forum for people to discuss and debate the merits of a project with the implicit goal of this being a constructive form of teamwork. They are frequently frustrated by the lack of response from their Asian colleagues, the seemingly mindless agreement with what they are suggesting, and the general lack of participation in discussions. This suggests a lack of interest and commitment to the Americans.

Conversely, Chinese are taught to take a humble approach in communication, offering hesitant responses as a way to both save face and maintain relationships. While they use the word "yes" to respond to a query as we have discussed at length previously, it has a myriad of meanings none of which may be agreement; furthermore the Chinese rarely use the word "no," choosing instead to use *"perhaps," "it's possible,"* or *"maybe"* to communicate a face-saving "no."[6]

In team meetings the Chinese members of the team will rarely disagree openly with a boss or colleague out of consideration for his or her position, and are unlikely to voice dissenting opinions in a public forum. It is not that they don't have an opinion; in fact, they may even have a dissenting view. It is just that restraint ensures the maintenance of harmony and saves the face of the person leading the conversation in the presence of others.[7]

Imagine the potential for miscommunication when the American colleague says to her Chinese colleague in a team meeting "So do you agree that this is possible?" and the Chinese colleague nods and says, "Perhaps, we could do it that way." The American hears, "we can do it," or assumes that the hesitancy reflects a noncommittal response, while the Chinese believes she has informed her American colleague that "it is not likely."

What is important to know is that in team meetings the Asian members of the team will rarely disagree openly with a boss or colleague out of consideration for his or her position, and are unlikely to voice dissenting opinions in a public forum. In each restrained culture there are a myriad of face-saving ways dissent is communicated. Another point to keep in mind is that speakers will not usually put themselves in a situation to lose face. Before presenting a new and possibly controversial idea at a "public" meeting, the person would have previously met with the attendees individually to present the ideas and get their buy-in. This way they would be able to count on the support of their colleagues, boss, or direct reports at the meeting.

## THE DILEMMA OF COMMUNICATING OUTCOMES: LINEAR AND CIRCULAR

Supporting their direct and expressive communication style, Americans are likely to deliver messages in a logical and matter of fact manner with the goal to drive the listener toward the desired result. Little imagination is necessary as the speaker states the desired outcome. This style is well suited to short-term task accomplishment, but quite limited in developing inclusive relationships or broadening views on a topic. Unexplored, the direct style of communication tends to give those from societies with more indirect communication patterns the impression of simplicity in thinking, a lack of awareness of the other person and may be experienced as arrogant.

Conversely, the Chinese drawing on their indirect and restrained communication style, will present information in a more circular fashion, allowing the listener to read between the lines and through reflection reach the conclusion to which the speaker is leading them. Indirect cultures speak around a topic using stories, metaphors, and analogies that guide the listener toward an outcome. The circular communication style is well suited for facilitating relational development and collaboration. Unexplored, the circular style is experienced by those who are from direct cultures as slow and indecisive.[7]

We selected American and Chinese examples to introduce you to the three dilemmas experienced when high-context and low-context cultures are working together. As the American and Chinese cultures tend to be on the opposite poles of this paradox it is easiest to articulate the differences of these dilemmas through examples contrasting their behavior. While the behavior of other cultures may or may not be as exaggerated as these two, you will find that behavior evidenced in the United States is experienced to various degrees in Canada, Great Britain, Scandinavia, Australia, and Western Europe.

The communication styles evidenced by the Chinese are generally experienced to various degrees in other Asian countries and across the Indian subcontinent. In these cultures the speaker's desire is to maintain harmony. Although expressiveness is a more prevalent dimension in African and South American communication, these cultures also place emphasis on relationship and tend toward circular and indirect communication.

## BERNARD, WAI TING, AND THE THREE DILEMMAS

As we have introduced the challenge of communicating effectively across cultures you have learned that a simple "yes" is not so simple when you are working with people from other cultures and that these other cultures, the high context ones, make up over 70% of the world's population. The incompatibility of the direct and indirect styles provides a fertile environment for misunderstandings and miscommunication. Add to this the non-portability of humor and sarcasm, and the challenges faced in communicating effectively across cultures may become monumental.

If this organization is to continue to enjoy the benefits these two high performers can bring, both employees will need to learn new ways of communicating that will allow each to work effectively and satisfactorily with the other. Both Bernard and Wai Ting will need to learn to speak and listen in new ways, finding a balance in the way they communicate together.

## COMMUNICATING IN THE "SPACE BETWEEN"

There are different ways to understand and frame communication. In the traditional (and direct) way of understanding messages that are communicated, responsibility for creating and interpreting messages is placed within each speaker in the conversation. Figure 4.3 represents this form of interaction. Person A wants to get something done and seeks the assistance of Person B. Based on her needs, Person A sends a message to Person B. The message reaches Person B, who hears and gives meaning to what Person A has said based on her experience of the world. Then Person B replies to Person A, who hears and gives meaning to the message based on her own experience of the world; and so the cycle continues. In this model, as in our illustration of the conversation between Bernard and Wai Ting, meaning is made within each individual and as a result there is greater opportunity for misunderstandings to occur.

Working successfully in a transnational environment, there needs to be a shared responsibility for ensuring the clarity of communication and creating shared meaning. For this to happen, communication needs to take place in the *space between* individuals in addition to *within*

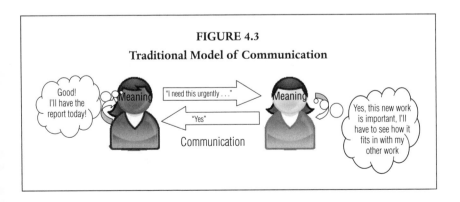

**FIGURE 4.3**

**Traditional Model of Communication**

Good! I'll have the report today!

Meaning — "I need this urgently . . ." — Meaning

"Yes"

Communication

Yes, this new work is important, I'll have to see how it fits in with my other work

each individual. This approach to communication has implications for the requisite skills and capabilities of transnational leaders. In communicating in the "space between" you enter into a conversation assuming that you are in the same moment as others, but having different experiences based on your "mental programming." Accepting that the frames of reference you use to process information are not the same as the other person, you begin to recognize the necessity for taking the time to speak *with* rather than *at* the other person.

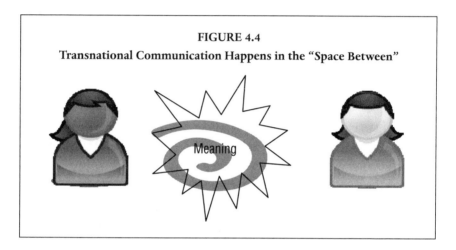

FIGURE 4.4
Transnational Communication Happens in the "Space Between"

Figure 4.4 illustrates the relationship that occurs in the "space between."

While the conversation between Bernard and Wai Ting might have happened in any number of ways in the "space between," one possibility is that the conversation may have gone like this:

**An Alternative Take on the Conversation**
**between Bernard and Wai Ting**

Bernard asked Wai Ting, one of the staff members on his team, to create an urgent report needed for an upcoming meeting he was having with his boss. Wai Ting listened to the request, and said, "Yes." Bernard realized that while "yes" in New York usually meant "yes, I'll do it right away" he had learned that in Singapore "yes" had many possible meanings. He looked at Wai Ting and said "I'm assuming that 'yes' means I'll have the report today."

Wai Ting looked serious and said with some surprise, "Today is difficult." She began to speak about two other projects for customers that were also due this week.

While wanting to quickly finish the conversation and move on, Bernard concentrated on listening to Wai Ting, taking the time to really hear what she was telling him. While he wasn't initially clear on what these other projects had to do with his request he focused his attention and thought about the messages she wanted him to take from the story: she was already busy with other important projects; the other projects were for customers and thus had priority.

When Wai Ting ended her explanation, Bernard acknowledged what she had said by saying "I can see that the time needed to create this report conflicts with two current projects. I can appreciate that, and wonder how this project might also be done this week?"

Wai Ting smiled, pleased that he had understood her dilemma. Wondering if he had any flexibility in his schedule, she said, "Well, since my section of the report needs to be integrated with sections that others are providing you, would it be possible to work on the report section by section? Wai Ting consulted her schedule and said, "I could have the data for the first section to you by tomorrow, and the data for the remaining two sections the following morning. Bernard said, "I can work with that schedule."

Perhaps as you reflected on the challenges of communicating "in the space between," you noted that the conversation took more time than you think you had to give or may typically give to this type of communication. It required Bernard to slow down his approach, to listen to a seemingly unrelated story and make sense of it, and check out the assumptions he was making as he gave meaning to Wai Ting's story. It required Wai Ting to acknowledge Bernard's listening and patience, address her concerns more directly than she would have traditionally, and take joint accountability for working effectively together. Most importantly, through this conversation the two developed a mutually satisfying alternative solution.

Taking shared responsibility for giving meaning in the "space between" and co-creating communication is highly effective in situations in which you are communicating across cultural differences.

While it does initially take more time it creates a space for understanding to occur and allows others to have voice. It increases the partnership as all parties work toward mutual success.

## THE TRANSNATIONAL LEADER, THE "SPACE BETWEEN," AND DIALOGUE

In the ever-growing complexity of today's global world, taking time to create meaning in the "space between" is important to the success of the transnational leader. The transnational leader's success is dependent on building an increased awareness of the three dilemmas on the communication continuum and developing competence to communicate and respond from any position. This continuum flows from one-directional to two-directional communication—from *command* to *discussion* to *dialogue* (Figure 4.5).

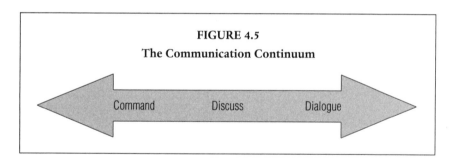

**FIGURE 4.5**
**The Communication Continuum**

Command          Discuss          Dialogue

American business communication patterns have traditionally been designed to minimize input and expedite output. Based on centuries of military leadership and strongly influenced by the mechanization of industry in the early twentieth century, a leader's communication has historically been planned to command and control both people and processes. Much of our present model of business is still based on an outmoded mechanistic model of organization with "people" simply considered an extension of the machinery.[8] In this model, thinking wasn't requisite, while taking direction was.

Post-World War II business structure shifted to support rapid growth and development. *Discussion* became an important form of leadership communication. The leader would state his or her view encouraging others to offer their perspectives with the goal being to have efficient and effective problem solving that would drive outcomes.

Communicating through *discussion* brought the voices of others into conversation in a controlled manner. In discussion, each person offers a solution and argues for its rationality. Listening to others is done to strengthen your claim and refute the other person's view. Rather than seeking to understand and build on others' thinking, discussion results in a more singular focus, with an expedited outcome based on the strength of your debate. While the aim of discussion is to construct the best possible solution, because of its argumentative nature, discussion may unknowingly limit innovation and creativity. That said, discussion is best used to manage day-to-day changes and time-limited situations. It is a particularly effective process to identify weak spots that need to be strengthened or corrected. It allows for targeted innovation in an efficient time period.

Moving the leadership conversation along the continuum from *discussion* to *dialogue* shifts the focus of communication away from solutions to exploratory conversations that clarify assumptions and ensure the expression of diversity of opinions. By design, dialogue is an expansive process that draws synergistically on the accumulated knowledge and experience of those present. By its very nature it slows down the decision-making process and provides for new ways of viewing a situation offering the potential for more universally innovative responses.

Because dialogue is an inherently slower process that brings groups circuitously toward shared solutions, it is best used at the start of projects to create shared vision and ownership, in assessment processes to consider the breadth and depth of experiences in generating creative and innovative outcomes, and in creating and implementing large scale change efforts where buy-in is essential and people are not likely to be won over only by well-stated arguments. The challenge to the transnational leader is to recognize which situations would benefit from discussion and which from dialogue.

Dialogue is a conversation in which each participant considers the others present and engages with them through collaboration. Drawing on the concept of making meaning in the "space between," dialogue provides a communication process to respectfully surface and embrace differences of opinion as the means to create success. The conversational flow of dialogue encourages deeper understanding of an individual's perspective, not to necessarily refute, but to view the world as the other person does. People in dialogue seek to elicit and understand the beliefs and assumptions that unconsciously guide responses. They look for the common ground between diverse opinions and integrate differences to free creativity and foster innovation. It is through the practice of dialogue that the more humane, personal side of being in a relationship takes center stage. The pace, level of mutuality and respect, and opportunity to express alternative points of view make it well suited for communication across difference.

## "LIVE" DIALOGUE

The four aspects of dialogue allowing for alternative behaviors, surfacing assumptions, and creating different relational dynamics are given the acronym *LIVE Dialogue* (Figure 4.6).

---

FIGURE 4.6
"LIVE" Dialogue

### L ? V <3

---

- *Listening* with openness to understand
- *Inquiry* with curiosity to learn
- *Voicing* our thoughts and feelings to be heard
- *Empathy* with respectful understanding of others

## Listening

While we all think we know what listening means and believe that we do it, in actual dialogue we are talking about being fully present to the other person and listening to understand their perspective. In this conversation, we are not seeking to disagree or find fault with the other person's logic; rather our goal is to reveal the assumptions underlying what is being said and to identify a common ground that exists between us where we can meet in collaboration. If we do this well we become better informed.

This approach to listening can be especially challenging when we disagree with the other person's logic because it differs from our own and we believe that we know better. It is also challenging when the other person does not express himself or herself in the same logical flow as we do, when their communication is less or more direct than we are accustomed to, and when their timing is faster or slower than our own.

> Responding from his frustration he cut her off and said to her, "Which part of the phrase "The report is urgent' didn't you understand?" Wai Ting became silent and looked down.

Wai Ting became silent because she knew from Bernard's response that he wasn't listening to her and that what she had to say was not valued. Bernard was frustrated because Wai Ting's comments about the different projects seemed to have nothing to do with his request and he was frustrated that she would even discuss something so unrelated during this important interchange. There were many assumptions being made on both their parts that could have been cleared up if they had slowed down the process and really listened to each other with the intention of understanding.

Transnational leaders can lead the way by modeling these skills and showing adaptability in communicating with their staff from different cultures. They need not be perfect nor always get it right, but the intention of listening respectfully will gain favor and support and will let others know of the value of the endeavor.

## Inquiry

We want to partner our use of the term inquiry with curiosity in that we encourage taking an exploratory approach to finding out more than what you hear or think you know.

Inquiry suggests we enter into conversations with curiosity. Children possess the gift of curiosity that as adults we seem to lose because we think we are supposed to have the answers. We can fashion ourselves as explorers trying to discover the unknown and unveil what is not yet apparent to solve the mystery. We can do this only if we acknowledge that there is more than what we currently know and we are eager to find out what is missing. This can be accomplished by asking for more information and probing as deep as is appropriate according to acceptable cultural parameters.

> Bernard realized that while "yes" in New York usually meant "yes, I'll do it right away" he had learned that in Singapore "yes" had many possible meanings. He looked at Wai Ting and said "I'm assuming that 'yes' means I'll have the report today."

Bernard took the time to check his understanding by confirming the meaning behind the comment Wai Ting had made. He had learned from too many miscommunications in the past that there are several ways to interpret what is being said. Wai Ting appreciated the opportunity to clarify what she had meant. Transnational leaders can model inquiry skills and, therefore, give permission to others to ask for clarification. This dispels any perception that they are expected to know the meaning of a potentially confusing statement and positively reinforces engaging in dialogue to ensure clarity.

## Voicing

The act of having voice is to have the power to say out loud what we want others to hear. To do this there are certain conditions that must be satisfied. We need to feel safe from criticism or reprisal, valued as a contributing member, and validated in that our ideas are considered seriously. The opposite of creating an atmosphere in which we feel comfortable having voice is being silenced. In situations in which we are silenced we are shut down because the conditions are not conducive to speaking and to sharing parts of ourselves. This is not to be confused with deliberately being silent, which is a conscious choice of communicating.

In our initial story of Bernard and Wai Ting, Bernard in his frustration and through his use of sarcasm unknowingly silences Wai Ting.

> Bernard was frustrated that the report wasn't ready and further baffled by Wai Ting's reply concerning another unrelated project. He knew he had been clear in his request. As a result of his frustration he cut her off and said to her, "Which part of the phrase 'The report is urgent.' didn't you understand?'" Wai Ting became silent and looked down.

Across time and a series of related incidents Wai Ting may come to believe that her voice is not heard and her input not valued. Her feelings of self-worth may be diminished, and in future circumstances she may not share valuable perspectives as she has lost her voice.

Having the opportunity to give voice is facilitated by leaders who provide that space and occasion; therefore the other side of having voice is that it requires leaders who value others' contributions and, therefore, create a space for others to share their thoughts, views, and feelings. There is recognition that people in the organization who have the opportunity to give voice to their concerns, ideas, and feelings will be more engaged and their personal involvement will lead to higher productivity than those whose voices are unheard.

While voice remains important across all cultures, there are important cultural implications that differentiate how this is fostered. While some cultures allow and even encourage employees to appropriately challenge the boss, in other cultures in which relationships are more hierarchical and positional power is more likely to be honored, giving voice to others becomes more complex. As a transnational leader, it is not initially realistic to expect that your staff will openly challenge you. In hierarchical cultures challenging your boss is done discretely and indirectly and never in the presence of an audience. That said, there are ways to encourage voice in public settings and to ensure that all have voice.

## Empathy

Empathy is being able to see a situation from another person's perspective or to be able to stand in someone else's shoes. Through empathy we are able to understand how and why people come to the beliefs they hold even if we do not share those beliefs. Empathy is the basis for feeling and showing compassion toward others. It is requisite to validate other people's comments and contributions.

Empathy is very challenging, for in certain situations it may be confused with agreement. What is important to know is that empathy requires understanding another's point of view. It does not require agreement or compliance. With empathy we acknowledge another's perspective and are then able to clarify our own point of view through this understanding.

> When Wai Ting ended her story and Bernard acknowledged what she had said by saying "I can see that this report conflicts with the work you are doing on the other project," Wai Ting nodded in agreement, pleased that he understood her dilemma. . . . Bernard then said, "What options would you propose?"

Small gestures that acknowledge another person's predicament can go far in building relationships. With empathy, trust and caring are being modeled, and in turn, others will collaborate with you because they believe that you have their best interest at heart.

To "LIVE" dialogue then requires being attendant to others and *listening* to what they have to say, using *inquiry* to gain insight into another person's needs or views, and in this process creating the space for *voice*. Listening, inquiry, and giving voice enables you to create the space to experience the world as another does with *empathy*. When you "LIVE" dialogue you are acting with *respect for others*.

In a cross-cultural context this assumes an even greater importance. Respect begins by appreciating the different mores, values, and beliefs that each person brings to the conversation. Rather than judging the way things are done from the standards learned in their country of origin, the transnational leader learns to observe, inquire, and integrate new information as an overlay to co-creating communication. There is an acknowledgment that while diversity in thinking, being, and doing adds richness to the organization, it is a challenge and a necessity to remain open and respectful of these differing views, creating a space in which others may be heard and appreciated.

There are some general norms of communication that can make dialogue difficult. Leaders who value the art of argument will find dialogue difficult. Leaders who work from a strong sense of urgency and a "just do it" orientation will be challenged to slow down the pace of the decision-making process. Conversely, those from cultures with norms that support reverence and obedience will find it unnatural to engage in inquiry as it may appear to be challenging those who are senior to them.

There are individual differences and cultural norms that govern how people participate in and contribute to conversations. Individual preferences may range from people jumping in and saying what is on their mind to those who want more time to reflect and need to be invited into the conversation. Communicating across cultures provides experiences that are potential opportunities for growth and development. In situations in which we are surprised to the point of being shocked and enraged, these are gems for learning if we have the mindset and tools to process them as such.

As we have explored in this chapter, the challenge of communicating across cultures is overshadowed by the benefits that can be reaped when this is done well. Transnational leaders may experience the tension of being true to their own instincts of communication, while at the same time trying to honor the varied communication styles at play within their multicultural teams. Being aware of this tension and understanding the consequences of whatever choices they make will enable these transnational leaders to be more in control of the communication flow and to work toward constructive outcomes. Using LIVE dialogue is one frame to consider in facilitating intercultural communication.

Figure 4.7 is a chart that can be used in planning your next transnational communication.

**FIGURE 4.7**

**Worksheet for Transnational Communication**

| Characteristic | Notes |
|---|---|
| Direct/Indirect ⟷ | |
| Discussion/Dialogue ⟷ | |
| Linear/Circular - ⟷ | |
| **L (listening)** <br> What do I need to listen for? <br> What do I need to do to show I am listening? <br> How can I make sure I am being listened to? | |
| **? (inquiry)** <br> What do I need to know? <br> How shall I frame my questions? <br> How can I ensure my questions are received openly? | |
| **V (voice)** <br> What do I need to do to ensure I allow the other person to have voice? <br> What do I need to do to ensure I have voice? | |
| **<3 (empathy)** <br> What do I need to be empathic about? <br> How can I show empathy? | |

# 5 | PARADOX OF ACTION: DOING AND REFLECTING

Doing                                                    Reflecting

*Workplaces are not typically associated with reflection. . . .*
*In the workplace reflection of any kind has been*
*considered a luxury. . . . Yet paradoxically, reflection is . . .*
*part of the lifeblood of organizations in today's*
*turbulent economic environment.*

—VICTORIA MARSICK[1]

## BALANCING ACTION AND THOUGHT

In this chapter we introduce the paradox of action, suggesting that to be an effective transnational leader requires a balance between action and thought—doing and being. While historically, some cultures embraced reflection, the business world draws from the "just do it" cultures that drive action without deep thought. In this chapter we discuss the following:

- Techniques to support effective doing with critical reflection
- Reflection in action and reflection on action
- Reflecting individually and in partnership

# HOW MUCH TIME DO YOU SPEND
# REFLECTING ON WHAT YOU ARE DOING?

When we ask this question to transnational leaders, no matter what their culture of origin, they look at us blankly. Thinking they may not have heard our question, we repeat ourselves asking again, "How much time did you spend this week reflecting on what you are doing?" Finally in each group a brave soul speaks out telling us, "We don't have time to think, we are working 10 (12 and 14) hours a day. The more we deliver, the more that needs to be done."

Being conscious of the need to get things done leaders with a Blackberry™ or iPhone™ usually have them on the table at the start of our workshop, hoping to be able to surreptitiously read and respond to messages as they arrive. One of our clients told us recently that no matter where he is in the world, the United States, Europe, or Asia, whenever he sends his boss an e-mail he has a response back in 5 minutes. He assumes his boss sleeps with the Blackberry on the night stand waking up each time it twills an incoming message: 200 e-mails a day, 2 minutes to read and 2 minutes to respond to half of those received. Do the math; advances in communication are driving action 24/7, but are we really getting anything done?

Operating at this pace takes a toll on us, limiting our effectiveness and impacting our health and well being over time. The analogy of a hamster running in its exercise wheel comes to mind. It is running at a faster and faster pace, but is never able to get off of the cylindrical treadmill unless it jumps off the side or falls off. As long as the hamster keeps running in the same direction no matter how fast it runs it will always be in the same place, expending energy but not reaching a destination.

The balancing of excessive doing is being. When we are too heavily engaged in a very active life of doing, we do not spend enough time reflecting on what it is we are actually doing. The risk here is that like the hamster, we get trapped into patterns of action that may not be productive and may or may not be in our best interests or the best interests of our organizations. Considering the complexity of the world today the transnational leader has a responsibility to actively ask, as Argyris suggests, "Why are we doing this?" and "Are we doing the right thing?"[2]

It is necessary to slow down our pace and take time to reflect on what we are doing and how we are accomplishing it and to identify the long-term effects of our actions. Without enough time to reflect on what we are doing, we may deprive ourselves of the time to reenergize, to let our creativity flourish, and to entertain alternative possibilities. And we may deprive our organizations of the knowledge and wisdom they sought when they hired us. It is also worthwhile to consider that driving action reflects a Eurocentric orientation and doesn't necessarily take into account the value of providing time for relationships to grow and be nurtured.

There are a variety of influences that may lead us to focus more on doing than being; these influences come from culture, religion, and spiritual practices, in addition to our work environments. Working across cultures creates situations that require us to critically reflect on their elements, determining how to be effective when working with others different from us.

As indicated through our examples, the standards of global business are weighted more heavily on the doing side of the continuum. Recognizing the needs of a more diverse pool of people and acknowledging the complexity of our times make it essential to balance this heavy emphasis on doing with being. For those from cultures which believe more strongly in individual agency in getting things done, there is trust in being able to accomplish what needs to be done and therefore the amount of doing continues to increase. This is a difficult pace to sustain and in a transnational setting it may be done at the cost of disengaging those who are more accustomed to integrating being into their lives and work practices.

There is the risk of alienating those with whom we need to work in partnership. Since each person on the team may have different approaches to how we do what needs to be done, and we bring different culturally influenced values to the table, the fervor to continuously produce does not allow time to reflect on how we can work more effectively collectively. For those from Eurocentric cultures this is partly the result of thinking as individual contributors and wanting to be star performers. Those acculturated in this manner want to rise to the occasion.

Those acculturated to working together as a member of a group with a focus on interdependence may struggle to work under these conditions. Disagreements may surface amongst teams working with these competing values and processes because of the pressure we allow ourselves to be put under and to which we put others. If there was more time initially to reflect on our work processes we would be able to utilize the diversity of our styles and input for better outcomes and processes.

The following case provides a work-based illustration of how one behavioral pattern of doing became an encumbrance to the Manager (Carla) and her employee (Mahmoud). Consider the impact that action without reflection had on these two individuals, their relationship, and the organization.

## THE IMPACT OF DOING: THE NEED FOR REFLECTING

---

### Conversation between Carla and Mahmoud

Scenario:
Carla was preparing to have a mid-year performance review with one of her direct reports, Mahmoud. After a good start in the first quarter Mahmoud's performance had been problematic in the second quarter and she was concerned because he has a prior history of erratic performance.

It was not easy for Carla to speak with Mahmoud as she often found him defensive. Whenever she would make a comment about his performance he would counter with an explanation as to why it turned out that way and he would usually blame another staff member, another department, or an external vendor. Carla wanted to be prepared for this conversation because she believed Mahmoud had the skills to be a stronger performer and needed him to become more constant in his performance. She dreaded the conversation and while her first thought was to delay it, she wanted to get it over with so they could move on.

As soon as Carla entered the room with Mahmoud she began the discussion by telling him a few positive things he had done for the team; she then told

---

him about all the performance issues and how he needed to improve. She knew she needed to begin with positive reinforcement because she had learned that in a management course she once attended. Carla then defined ways in which she thought Mahmoud should improve his performance.

Carla wanted to get the meeting over with as quickly as possible and she didn't want to allow time for Mahmoud to counter her comments with excuses. She just wanted him to get on with it. As Carla spoke and Mahmoud had no chance to speak, he slumped deeper into his chair and looked down. At the end of the 10 minutes, Carla mentioned that she knew Mahmoud could rise to the occasion and that she was counting on him. When she asked him if that was understood and did he have any questions, Mahmoud shrugged his shoulders and said "Fine."

Mahmoud was dreading this meeting with Carla. In the past, she seemed very critical of him and he felt she blamed him for results that were out of his control. There were many tasks he was being asked to accomplish that he felt he was not authorized to complete; and when others disregarded him and did not comply Carla blamed him. He did not feel that she supported him and he wanted more direction. She kept asking him what he thought; however, he didn't think it was his place to offer ideas of how the team should proceed. That was clearly the charge of the leader and if she was not qualified to make these decisions and prepare others to execute them, then perhaps she should not be in charge.

This conversation between Carla and Mahmood follows a typical pattern of their interaction. It can be looked at from many angles and we would like you to consider the probing questions in Figure 5.1 as you make sense of it for yourself.

**FIGURE 5.1**

**Probing Questions for the Conversation between Carla and Mahmoud**

- What took place between Carla and Mahmoud?
- What was the level of commitment from Mahmoud?
- What was the level of support from Carla?
- What were Carla's goals for this conversation? Did she achieve them?
- What were Mahmoud's goals for this conversation? Did he achieve them?

Carla's goal was to get Mahmoud to improve his performance. As his manager she was responsible for providing him with the feedback he needed to make improvements in how he performed his job. She therefore took immediate action so as not to let this downturn in his performance continue to develop into something bigger. She needed results quickly and since she was responsible for reaching certain target goals, Mahmoud needed to deliver his targets. Carla simply did not have the time or patience to listen to his reasons or explanations, since at the end of the day it wouldn't bring about the results she needed for the team.

What does Carla really know about Mahmoud and his thoughts on the situation? Actually, Carla knows very little because she has framed Mahmoud's comments as excuses not worthy of discussion. Hence Carla does not take the time to talk to Mahmoud, to discover his concerns, and to understand why he makes the statements he does and why he finds fault with others. Carla is not aware of the impact her feedback has on Mahmoud or of how he perceives their interaction.

Carla has achieved great success in her career and she has done so by producing results. She is the person the organization goes to when they want to get things done. Carla is very heavily focused on the doing side of the continuum and since she has been successful she doesn't realize the value or the need to move toward the being side. Carla has been evaluated and rewarded as an individual contributor and this reinforces her continuing to work in this manner.

Mahmoud is disheartened and frustrated by the conversation with Carla. Mahmoud's educational background and life experiences have been in environments in which an individual's level of contribution is measured by rank and position. He is clearly junior to Carla and does not feel comfortable participating in the decision-making processes the way Carla expects him to do. He does expect that as his higher up, she will guide him and be responsible for his development and success because it will be a reflection on her.

Mahmoud does not believe that he has the positional authority to carry out some of the tasks Carla has charged him with fulfilling. When results do not come and other decisions need to be made he believes that Carla should make those decisions that change the course of direction. Based on his prior experience Mahmoud believes that these decisions are beyond the scope of his authority and power within the organization.

## POINTS TO CONSIDER

There are several points to consider (Figure 5.2) on this continuum of doing and reflecting to better understand the dynamics of what took place in this interaction between Carla and Mahmoud (Figure 5.3). We would like to introduce a few concepts here and interpret what took place through the lenses of these concepts.

---

**FIGURE 5.2**

**Points to Consider**

- On action
- In action
- Assumptions
- Meta-view

- Freeze Frame
- Intent vs. Impact
- Unintended Consequences

---

**FIGURE 5.3**

**On Action**

*On Action*—This is when we take the time to reflect on an action that has already been completed. We reflect on it by reviewing what has taken place and whether we achieved our objectives, what the outcomes were, what the next steps are, and so on. The purpose of this review is to identify what worked well and what needs to be improved for further learning and growth opportunities.

---

In our scenario with Carla and Mahmoud we learned that there was a pattern in their relationship that was not leading to positive outcomes. Carla reflected on her past interactions with Mahmoud and determined that quickly delivered directive feedback would be more productive in this performance meeting. She accepted his "fine" as agreement and ended the meeting. Unfortunately, Carla may be mistaking Mahmoud's complicity and silence for acceptance. His performance may continue on satisfactorily, but it may be coming out of compliance and not commitment and much may be lost from not engaging Mahmoud more thoroughly. Mahmoud does not feel it is his place nor does he have the authority to challenge Carla. As a leader, she is supposed to know this and be more perceptive about the meaning of his silence.

If Carla were to slow down her process, allowing herself more time to reflect on their past interactions (reflecting on action) and think about her role in contributing to their dynamics, she may be more inclined to structure her next conversation with Mahmoud in a way that would take his concerns into consideration, and likely lead to more productive outcomes. By focusing on expediency, Carla is going fast at the beginning; however, she will likely have to go slow later when her future working relationship with Mahmoud becomes further impaired.

Like many leaders Carla is on the doing side of the continuum; she would benefit from moving further toward the being side as she gives herself time to set things up in a way that will be more beneficial to all. As the supervisor she has the power in this relationship and it is up to her to create a setting in which Mahmoud will feel more comfortable and able to express his concerns and expectations. Carla needs to understand that although she expects someone junior to her to speak up because she is providing that opportunity; it is not part of Mahmoud's heritage. What Carla would view as being independent and showing agency, Mahmoud would view as insolence and disrespect.

Mahmoud wants to be a good performer and he wants to please Carla, as she is his boss. What Carla has labeled as his "erratic performance" is possibly rooted in his beliefs and assumptions about work and the roles and responsibilities of the boss and the subordinate. Because Carla has not asked Mahmoud to clarify his thoughts, needs, or ambitions, Mahmoud is discouraged. When he previously tried to explain the circumstances to her she did not appear to listen or understand him, generally silencing him and not providing a forum to discuss the factors at play.

Mahmoud expects Carla to know what he wants because she is his supervisor and his definition of a competent supervisor is someone who knows what is best for her staff. Mahmoud needs to realize that because he and Carla are from different cultures and have had different living and work experiences, there is a good chance that their expectations of a supervisor–direct report relationship may differ. As challenging as it may be for Mahmoud to make his expectations known to Carla, he will need to find a way to have more voice so that he and Carla can have a more productive working relationship.[3]

---

**FIGURE 5.4**

**In Action**

*In Action*—This is when we become more aware of our actions as we are performing them and are able to view them from an outside vantage point, almost taking a meta-perspective from an elevated external location. Many times we are aware that the anticipated course of action is not happening, yet we are too caught up in the content to be able to discern what needs to be done differently. Reflecting in action provides us with the ability to reflect on the process of what we are doing as we are doing it, and make a change if we so desire.

---

At any point in the discussion Carla was having with Mahmoud she had the opportunity to verify if the conversation was progressing as planned. If she had been skilled enough to reflect in action (Figure 5.4) and recognize that she was not obtaining his agreement, she could have adjusted her approach to shift the conversation to the desired path. She could have asked Mahmoud questions that would be likely to engage him, or she could have openly stated that the meeting was not going as she had planned, allowing Mahmoud another opportunity to discuss the situation. Mahmoud could also have reflected on the dynamic of their interaction and since it did not meet his needs or expectations and was following a repeatedly destructive path could have asked for time to slow down the pace and perhaps change the direction of the conversation. He could have found a way to express his support of Carla and at the same time some of his frustrations in the workplace that he felt were beyond his control. Both parties would need to step outside of their culturally created comfort zones to adjust their styles to the style of the other.

Typically, this is very challenging to do although not impossible. We tend to get so involved in what we are saying and what we want as a result of the interaction that we lose sight of the process. We are focused on the *"what"* and not the *"how."* Practicing by becoming better at reflection on action will aid us in being able to be in the moment and be better at reflecting in action.

---

**FIGURE 5.5**

**Assumptions**

*Assumptions*—We have past experiences, which cause us to create expectations about ourselves, other people and the situations within which we find ourselves. These expectations may or may not come to life. It is a normal procedure we go through as humans, which suits us well for our survival. The issue is when we do not realize that we are making assumptions and we take them to be the Truth (the overarching Truth with a capital T). In the situations in which our expectations are not met we may become confused, disappointed and angry. We are typically not consciously aware where these feelings are arising from and the challenge is to surface these assumptions and make them explicit. Once they are surfaced we are able to address them to confirm whether they are true.

---

In the exchange between Carla and Mahmoud, both were probably operating from a preconceived set of assumptions about the other person (Figure 5.5). Carla assumed that Mahmoud was not dependable because of his inconsistent performance, because he didn't take responsibility for his actions, because he blamed others for his problems, and because she did not perceive him to be a team player. Mahmoud assumed that Carla cared only about results and didn't care about him as a person, that she was looking for someone to blame and it was often him, that she had favorites on the team, and, finally, that her only interest was in how she appeared to her bosses.

What we hear is filtered through these assumptions, which distort the message and cloud the intent. Carla's real concern may be the team and everyone on it, not just herself. She may want to better support Mahmoud and the team and may be looking to them to suggest ways in which she can be helpful. This is what she has been developed to expect about how teams function in the workplace. However, based on their cultural backgrounds, her team members may not be comfortable asking for her support. They may expect her to provide the needed support because the leader should know what they need.

Mahmoud's explanations may be signs of his frustration at not being able to access the information he needs to perform his tasks. His perception is that he lacks authority to access it himself, and that he is telling Carla that he needs her support. Yet the comments are perceived to be negative, reinforcing previous assumptions; and so the cycle continues.

One way out of this is to stop and ask "what assumptions am I making?" and "are the assumptions I hold accurate across cultures?" (Figure 5.6). The leader can therefore check and maintain them if they serve a purpose and discard them if they get in the way of communication and productive teamwork. Assumptions can serve as a survival mechanism and short cut, or they may be a hindrance.

---

FIGURE 5.6

Meta-View

*Meta-View*—When we are engaged in an activity we are usually very absorbed in the content part of it. Rarely do we take a step back while engaged to consider the process. Using the metaphor of perching on a bird's nest to view the scene below, we can have a much wider and more inclusive view of any given situation. Taking a meta-view of a situation, therefore, means that while we are still interacting in a particular situation, we are also perched on the bird's nest looking down at what we are doing. This allows us to observe the process within which we are engaged.

---

In the interaction between Carla and Mahmoud, Carla felt the tension in the conversation and knew that it was not going as she had hoped. Carla was caught up in the content of the conversation and was thinking about her goal of getting Mahmoud to be a better team player; she also wanted to get her points across before Mahmoud had a chance to refute them. She missed an opportunity to bridge the gap in understanding between herself and Mahmoud because she was not paying attention to what was going on in the *dynamic* of the conversation.[4] Her attention was on what she needed to say and what Mahmoud needed to do.

This is not an unusual interaction; rather it is one that occurs on a daily basis between people working in organizations. This is especially true when interactions occur between people of different cultures who experience performance management sessions in different ways. There are different expectations concerning the role of the boss and the direct report related to how direct or indirect the communication can and should be and on the role of accountability in augmenting change. If Carla had slowed the process down and checked the process of the conversation, the dynamic between them, and Mahmoud's presence and participation, she would have realized that her strategy was ineffective.

Mahmoud, on the other hand, also missed opportunities to be a more active participant in this conversation. He became a passive participant by not speaking up and giving voice to his concerns. It was not his custom to disagree openly with his boss, as that would be disrespectful. He believed that he was being falsely accused of underperforming, that his efforts were good, and that the lack of results was outside of his control. He had wanted to share this with Carla. He did feel it was his duty to deliver results, but without authority and the support of his boss and colleagues he didn't know how to make things happen.

If Mahmoud had taken a meta-view of the conversation they were having, he would have seen that Carla was concerned about the team's ability to honor their commitments. He might have seen that his silence might have been interpreted as insolence and that his concern was not evident as he kept his eyes lowered. Mahmoud would then have understood that although it might be uncomfortable for him, Carla was expecting him to be a more active participant on the team. He might begin this interaction by providing constructive insight into his dilemma and by being specific in indicating the type of support he needed from Carla to enable him to get his work completed successfully (Figure 5.7).

---

**FIGURE 5.7**

**Freeze Frame**

*Freeze Frame*—If we picture our interactions as a series of frames as in a movie, then we can also borrow from movies the ability to stop an action mid-frame. The purpose of this in the movies is for a character to get in place or to make something happen while time stands still for others. In our interactions sometimes the course of action does not always go according to plan. In those moments if we could, metaphorically, freeze frame, we would be able to either retake the scene or change direction to have it go in a more desirable path.

---

Carla felt the conversation was not going the way she had hoped and there were several points in the interaction at which she could have changed the course of the conversation. At the pace the conversation was moving the conversation was turning into a snowball rolling out of control. Carla dreaded encountering what she perceived to be Mahmoud's resistance, so she unsuccessfully tried to regain control of the conversation. Because Mahmoud never fully participated in the conversation he had no control over its direction.

The snowball effect might have been stopped if Carla had taken a step back and asked an open question to draw Mahmoud into the conversation. This would have increased the balance of the participation, slowed the pace of talking, created an opportunity for listening, and balanced the sources of information. As long as Carla was doing all the talking it was a one-sided conversation. Carla could only guess at what was going on in Mahmoud's mind because she didn't give him the opportunity to voice any of his views or concerns. Mahmoud, on the other hand, relinquished his voice to Carla, as he did not try to contribute to the conversation. If both of them thought about the conversation as an opportunity for mutual sharing, a partnership, they could have regained control of the flow and pace of the discussion and stopped the discussion from running out of control. They were caught in the action of "doing" the conversation rather than "reflecting" on the conversation — what was happening as compared to what they wanted to happen (Figure 5.8).

---

**FIGURE 5.8**

**Intent versus Impact**

*Intent vs. Impact*—We have intentions for a certain outcome and at times we achieve that outcome. In those cases we can say that the impact we have on others and the situation is in alignment with our intent. At other times we do not accomplish what we intended and at those times we say that our intent and impact is not in alignment. One point to reflect on is this alignment and whether we are achieving what our intentions are or whether our intentions are not being satisfied because our behavior and actions are causing a different impact than we wanted. We can assess this because the reaction or response we get from others after our actions, differ from what we anticipated and this is due to the misalignment between our intention and the resulting impact of our behavior.

---

In the interaction between Carla and Mahmoud, Carla's intention was to help Mahmoud improve his performance in the workplace and be a more effective team member. She wanted to do it in as expeditious a way as possible because she didn't believe she could effectively manage the interpersonal dynamics between them, especially if Mahmoud challenged what she had to say. Carla wanted to get right to the point and since she believed she knew how she wanted Mahmoud to improve, she made suggestions to him about how he could change. She didn't ask his opinion about the situation.

Mahmoud interpreted her actions and comments as very directive, leaving him little choice but to comply with her wishes. She was his boss, she had the authority, and she did not seem interested in his take on the situation. Mahmoud didn't challenge Carla because as his boss she seemed so determined to get him to behave in a certain manner; he thought it rude to do anything else. Carla understood Mahmoud's response as one of compliance bordering on insolence as he shrugged his shoulders, looked down and said "fine."

We need to remember that our interpretation of the behaviors of others is based on our own lenses or filters, which often differ from those of the other people involved. Carla and Mahmoud both initiated and responded to each other based on their own frames of thinking and the impact they intended was not the impact their behavior actually produced (Figure 5.9). One way of checking this is to monitor the response and query the other person as to his or her understanding. The listener can also paraphrase back to the speaker what she or he understood and together they can see if the intent and impact are in alignment. If they are in alignment, then they can continue, knowing that their communication is in sync. If they are not in alignment it is time to make adjustments in the communication before further misunderstandings ensue.

---

**FIGURE 5.9**

**Unintended Consequences**

*Unintended Consequences*—There are times when our actions stimulate other actions to occur that we had not intentionally planned. Some of these may be positive side effects that are generated by all parties being in alignment with one another and benefiting from the interaction. At other times there is a snowball effect and whatever we do seems to wreak more havoc in ways that we didn't anticipate. Anticipating these possible side effects and exploring what they might be will help increase our preparedness to manage them, so that we can channel our efforts into more constructive outcomes.

---

Carla's intention in her conversation with Mahmoud was to obtain better performance results. If Mahmoud takes his frustration and negativity back to his team the issue is no longer be confined to Carla and Mahmoud. This is an unintended consequence that Carla may not have anticipated and one that she will want to avoid.

Carla has an image of what a team is, how it should function, and what her role as leader should be, while Mahmoud may have a different understanding of team and Carla's relation to it. Cultural orientations to teams play a role here in that in addition to the roles the members and leaders play, there are different expectations as to how communication is conducted, how decisions are made, and how strategy and its implementation are decided. Carla's understanding is that her role is to set the direction for the team and the role of the team members is to carry out the tasks. The team members can propose ways in which they would like to fulfill these tasks and Carla will approve or modify their suggestions. Mahmoud agrees that the leader, Carla, sets the direction of the team and determines how the tasks should be carried out; he does not believe he has the authority to determine such important steps.

Here is where there is potential confusion leading to unintended consequences. Carla expects Mahmoud to play a more active role in setting up the tasks for the team based on the strategy decided. Carla would even listen to his suggestions about how to shape the strategy if she thought they added value.

Mahmoud expects Carla to determine the strategy because she is in a higher position of authority and has more experience than him. He expects to be developed to fulfill the tasks as required, to eventually move into a role such as Carla's, and to move up in rank as he matures in the organization.

Carla is frustrated with Mahmoud's seeming lack of initiative and Mahmoud is frustrated with Carla's seeming lack of empathy and support. This paradox of action can be remedied if both persons are willing to slow down "doing" and move the focus to "being," allowing time and space to develop mutual understanding. It is the leader's role to create a non-threatening atmosphere that allows this conversation to take place. This is usually an initiative that starts with the leader. It is important to keep in mind the ingredients needed to create a comfortable atmosphere, as in a multicultural environment we may all have different wants and needs.

## QUADRANTS OF REFLECTION

Victoria Marsick, a leading international consultant, recognized the importance of reflection in 1990, as we noted in a quote we borrowed from her at the opening of this chapter. Imagine how much more fast-paced and complex the world has become since her call to reflection, and still we have not created the space to both "act" and to "reflect."

We believe that in the current and future milieu leaders must be prepared to reflect in action and on action, both individually or with another party in a one-on-one partnership or with several others in a group setting. The following approach provides a process as well as suggestions for how this can best be done

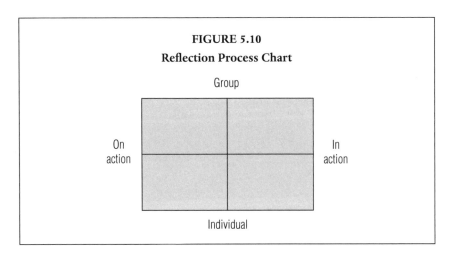

**FIGURE 5.10**
**Reflection Process Chart**

Group

On
action

In
action

Individual

There are five guiding questions that can be used in these quadrants (Figure 5.10) with slight variations depending on whether the reflection is taking place during an action or after it is completed, individually or in partnership. Each of these questions can be thought about and addressed in culturally sensitive ways as discussed.

## QUADRANTS OF REFLECTION WITH FIVE GUIDING QUESTIONS

The quadrants of reflection are shown in Figure 5.11.

**FIGURE 5.11**

**Quadrants of Reflection Chart with Guiding Questions**

GROUP

|  |  |
|---|---|
| 1. What worked well and how did we benefit?<br>2. What assumptions did we make?<br>3. What can we do differently?<br>4. What challenges did we face?<br>5. What did we do to overcome them? | 1. What is working well and how are we benefiting?<br>2. What assumptions are we making?<br>3. What can we do differently?<br>4. What challenges are we facing?<br>5. What are we doing to overcome them? |
| 1. What worked well and how did I benefit?<br>2. What assumptions did I make?<br>3. What can I do differently?<br>4. What challenges did I face?<br>5. What did I do to overcome them? | 1. What is working well and how am I benefiting?<br>2. What assumptions am I making?<br>3. What can I do differently?<br>4. What challenges am I facing?<br>5. What am I doing to overcome them? |

ON ACTION (left)    IN ACTION (right)

INDIVIDUAL

# CULTURAL IMPLICATIONS
# OF THE QUESTIONS

*Question 1:* How we *benefit* from a situation is directly linked to what we value, which is developed in the context of our cultures, however we define them. If we value autonomy and we feel as though we can act autonomously then we are likely to feel we are benefiting from a particular situation. In focusing on group level questions we can be made aware of how others benefit from the situation and assess whether that is similar to or different from how we benefit; adjustments can then be made accordingly.

*Question 2:* We are making explicit our implicit *assumptions*, which are directly linked to our cultures as well. We have been conditioned to expect a certain response to actions we take and when these responses are forthcoming we pay little attention to them. However, receiving responses that differ from what we expect provides an opportunity to pause and reflect on the assumptions we held that led to those expectations. Likewise, we have an opportunity to ponder the assumptions of our partners in conversation and to see what behaviors they had anticipated from us.

*Question 3:* If there is alignment between the expected outcome and the actual outcome we can either function in the same way or we can enhance what we did to obtain an even better outcome. If there is a lack of alignment with what we anticipated and what actually happened, we can take a step back and ask ourselves what we could have done *differently* to achieve the anticipated desired outcome. It is helpful to engage in this from the standpoint of curiosity, which will open up our creative channels, rather than the standpoint of judgment, which may inhibit us. We need to take into consideration the other party's values so we can ensure better alignment between our actions and their responses.

*Question 4:* We may face *challenges* when making changes simply because we are doing something differently from they way we normally do. These challenges may vary in intensity from minor adjustments to major overhauls. Our approaches stem from the way we have been acculturated, which involve our homes, communities, or organizations, if we think of organizational culture as one type of culture. It is useful to ask these questions because it can help us anticipate what may be ahead and enable us to be better prepared to deal with whatever comes our way.

*Question 5:* In this question we ask ourselves to be strategic in engaging in efforts to *overcome* any potential obstacles we face. We may rely on strategies and approaches that have been helpful to us in the past and we may also need to "think outside the box" and engage in approaches that are new to us. Having multiple ways to approach the situation, which can come from entertaining various cultural viewpoints, allows us to be better prepared to select the approach that is most appropriate at the time. Anticipating and understanding that reactions to our actions may result in unintended consequences because of differing cultural expectations will help us tailor our approaches in the most culturally sensitive ways.

We can now look at each quadrant in a bit more detail.

## ON ACTION: INDIVIDUAL

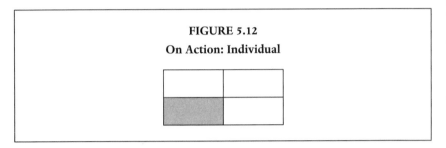

**FIGURE 5.12**
On Action: Individual

For a visual depiction of "on action: individual," see Figure 5.12.

1.  What worked well and how did I benefit?
2.  What assumptions did I make?
3.  What can I do differently?
4.  What challenges did I face?
5.  What did I do to overcome them?

These questions begin with an appreciative focus to allow us to capture the positive aspects of our interaction. We do this so that we may be equipped with ideas and techniques to apply to future interactions, as they have already proven successful. It also draws our attention to whether the goals we set for this interaction have been met. Overall, getting into the habit of reflecting on our experiences provides us the chance to learn and create paths for improvement. Assessing whether our impact and intentions are in alignment allows us to make adjustments so that we will be better equipped to face life's challenges. We will have thought through potential obstacles and we will have strategies to employ that have worked well for us in the past.

There are people who are from cultures in which self-praise is discouraged and the practice of identifying our own accomplishments may be uncomfortable. This exercise is not designed to make us self-centered, but rather to identify strategies and techniques that will enable us to be more effective contributors. Framing it in this manner may make it easier to engage in this type of reflection. If we are from more collectivist-oriented cultures we can think of it as a way of examining how our contributions helped the team achieve its goals, so that we can continue to be highly contributing members.[5] For more achievement-oriented cultures the purpose is the same.[6]

## ON ACTION: GROUP

For a visual depiction of "on action: group," see Figure 5.13.

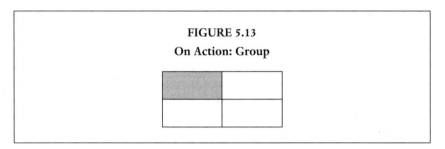

**FIGURE 5.13**
**On Action: Group**

Some of us take on the responsibility of thinking about what happens in our groups and what we need to do to make things better. This could be because we are in leadership roles and realize that one role of a leader is to take on the burdens of the group. This is not a faulty way of thinking; however, it does place an unfair burden on the person who carries the weight of the group. It also denies the group an opportunity to learn and grow together as they would be able to do in a group reflection process.

One way of addressing this is to engage in a group rather than an individual reflection process as a way of debriefing a joint rather than an individual effort. The guiding questions are as follows:

1.   What worked well and how did we benefit?
2.   What assumptions did we make?
3.   What can we do differently?
4.   What challenges did we face?
5.   What did we do to overcome them?

Starting with an appreciative tone allows the group members to begin to feel at ease and more comfortable in disclosing their feelings and concerns. It also allows people to feel good as they are being recognized for their contributions. For those from more achievement-oriented cultures, this activity will be more comfortable and the acknowledgment of good performances amongst the team members can be a way of building relationships, which in turn increases the trust and level of comfort the members experience. The second question clears up any misunderstandings that may exist within the group or between groups as we reveal the underlying assumptions that were governing our actions and our reasons for taking those actions. It also better prepares us to work as a team so that we get into the habit of questioning the reasons behind recommended actions so that all are clear about the factors motivating those actions. The third, fourth, and fifth questions prepare us to interact as a group and present chances for the group to build on the collective strengths of its members in meeting the identified challenges and moving forward to success.

Getting into the habit of reflecting as a group provides us the chance to strengthen our ties and become a "team" for future efforts. We can bring into play all the different attributes of the members and utilize these contributions in a way that benefits the group, the individuals in the group, as well as the organization. It raises our performance to a higher level as it covers any potential gaps that may have gone unnoticed.

## IN ACTION: INDIVIDUAL

For a visual depiction of "in action: individual," see Figure 5.14.

**FIGURE 5.14**
**In Action: Individual**

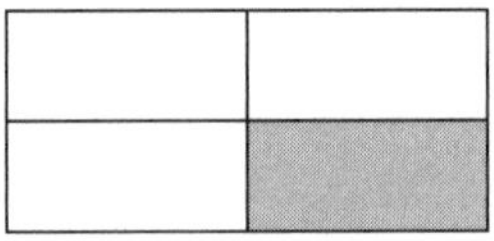

As we master the art of being able to reflect on actions we have completed, the next step is to bring these reflections into play earlier in the interaction. In this event, we would be reflecting in action, while the action is occurring. Being able to do this enables us to monitor ourselves so that we can make adjustments to the course of action we are taking as we are moving along instead of when it is all over. We would be able to address unintended consequences that might be occurring so that we can improve our chances at more satisfactory outcomes. This increases our level of cultural sensitivity as we pay attention to the other parties and monitor their reactions to what is taking place. We can query them when their reactions are not positive or we do not understand their responses.

There are two techniques to assist us in this endeavor. The first is to take a *meta-view*, which allows us to see ourselves from a third party vantage point as we are interacting. In utilizing this view we are able to monitor both the process and the content of our engagement. This allows us to identify times when we may not like the direction we are taking because the response we are getting is different from what we expected. We may then employ the second technique, which is to *freeze frame* the situation we are in and to decide to either retain the same course of action or to make a change. We are able to either roll back the tape and start anew or take a path different from the one toward which we have been veering.

In the freeze frame moment we may also want to ask the following questions to guide our reflection:

1.  What is working well and how am I benefiting?
2.  What assumptions am I making?
3.  What can I do differently?
4.  What challenges am I facing?
5.  What am I doing to overcome them?

We do a periodic mood check to determine that all is well when we freeze frame the action and take a meta-view. At this time we may also decide to continue reflecting individually or to bring the other parties into the reflection process, as described below.

## IN ACTION: GROUP

For a visual depiction of "in action: group," see Figure 5.15.

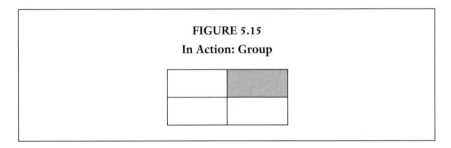

**FIGURE 5.15**
**In Action: Group**

We might go through a reflective process by ourselves as we take a meta-view of the situation within which we find ourselves; however, we may also want to include the group of which we are a member. As mentioned previously, a group process affords the members an opportunity to learn and grow together and to become a more effective team. Using the technique of freeze frame to pause all actions engages the team members in the added activity of assessing whether collectively they are on target with their goals, and if not, how they might make adjustments so that their intention and their impact are in alignment.

It asks the group members to be accountable and to share in the responsibility of taking a meta-view to observe the process as well as the content with which they are working. Stopping the process mid-way can be structured into the proceedings or can be done whenever any group member feels the need to have everyone examine the process.

1.   What is working well and how are we benefiting?
2.   What assumptions are we making?
3.   What can we do differently?
4.   What challenges are we facing?
5.   What are we doing to overcome them?

As a group we now explicitly confirm what is working well and how all the members are benefiting. One important point is that the group does not need to be in agreement on how the group's actions affect each member. Every person experiences the group differently and as a group it is critical to honor each person's experience of the situation as valid, even if it does not match our own experience. In revealing the members' assumptions the group has a chance to better understand the reasoning behind the actions as well as the comments of particular members and the impact they have on the group. It allows the group to make explicit the dynamics by which it is operating and how each person's actions impact the actions of the others. In doing this, the group can decide what adjustments need to be made and then how those adjustments may impact what is already underway. There may be some initial resistance or unintended consequences as a result of these changes and the group will need to decide how to manage these challenges.

The act of reflection slows down the process from the typically frenetic pace of doing business in the world today. We need this change of pace to be better prepared to make a difference that will benefit all involved. Many of us are "doers" and are leaning heavily on the doing side of the continuum; for these people changing to a slower pace may be an uncomfortable experience. At the same time it is a welcome change for those who naturally have a more reflective nature and feel as though that side of them has been less present because they are always trying to catch up with the doers.

## LEADER'S ROLE

As a leader it is important to continue to let our teams know that results are important in measuring success as they directly impact the organization's performance and its bottom line. At the same time, considering the paradox of action and the ends of the continuum of doing and being, we implore you to consider a more balanced approach to life in the fast lane. The demands placed on us as we continue operating in the twenty-first century will only increase as the pace at which we are expected to function gets faster. We can admire our technological advances and the ways in which we have become more and more efficient. The challenge is becoming more efficient without losing sight of the toll it may take on our interpersonal relationships and long-term performance. The expediency of satisfying short-term goals may in fact impede our progress in trying to sustain this long term.

It is therefore critical that transnational leaders acknowledge that reflection is a critical part of how business is conducted in the organization. We fully acknowledge that doing is important and at the same time we acknowledge that being is equally important; our individual and collective challenge is to balance the tension between the two perceived competing ends of the continuum. By considering the opposite ends of the continuum as supportive of each other rather than as competitive, we may make it easier to afford ourselves the time to engage in reflecting.

This of course is given more credence when the leader models the desired behaviors by engaging in the practices described in the preceding sections. In addition, it can be done by providing opportunities for people to learn and practice the skills both individually and as members of their group. By acknowledging this importance and engaging others in promoting these practices we show sensitivity to the different values and styles of engagement of the people with whom we work. The doing model of business has taken a stronger hold on business practices in the global arena; however, as more members of different cultures work together, it is time to incorporate practices that embrace the being end of the continuum as well. The pace of all doing and little being is not sustainable if we want to move forward in a healthy and productive way.

## SUGGESTED TIPS

- Carry the reflective questions around with you so that practicing them becomes a habit.
- Build in time for individual and group reflection as part of group work, including team meetings.
- Practice doing reflection "on action" with the goal of integrating this real time to become "in action" as well.

- Examine your assumptions to better understand why you operate the way you do and to attain deeper self-awareness.
- Practice freeze framing and taking a meta-view to hone your observational skills.
- Consider unintended consequences that may arise from your actions, especially when the intent and impact are not in alignment.

# 6 | PARADOX OF RESPONSE: SHORT TERM AND LONG TERM

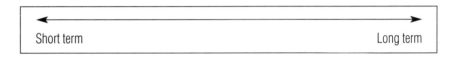

Short term                                                     Long term

*The significant problems we face cannot be solved
at the same level of thinking we were at when we created them.*

—ALBERT EINSTEIN

- Time orientation
- Time perspective
- Work and life balance

As we introduce you to the fifth and final paradox of transnational leadership we find ourselves returning to the theme that we began with in the Introduction. In transnational settings our lives are operating at a faster pace than ever before and work and life have become intricately interwoven.

It is in this setting that there is an increased demand for us to produce results in decreasing time frames. The global marketplace operates 24/7 and there is reason to be awake at all hours of the day and night to produce for someone somewhere in the world. To ensure our accessibility we give up "down time" and have little opportunity to truly get away from the hustle and bustle of our work for rest and relaxation with our spouses, children, family, and friends.

It is within this scenario that we introduce the paradox of response considering the dilemmas of short-term and long-term orientation. This continuum reviews the cultural impact on time orientation and recognizes that time is lived differently in different locations of the world. In discussing this paradox, we consider time orientation, time perspective, and time focus.

## TIME ORIENTATION AND TIME PERSPECTIVE

Culture has a significant impact on *time orientation*. It is important for transnational leaders to develop an awareness and understanding of how *time orientation* impacts people and organizations. Perhaps the success of the Swiss in creating the world's finest watches relates to their fascination with being "on time." If a meeting is to start at 2:00 pm a Swiss manager arrives at 1:50 pm as this ensures that she is on time. In India, if a team dinner is announced for 7:00 pm, it is useful to understand that food will likely be served at or after 10:00 pm and team members will only arrive after 8:00 pm or later.

*Time perspective* describes the tension that exists between cultures focused on satisfying short-term or longer-term goals and needs. Business coming from a Eurocentric orientation historically has taken a view toward immediate short-term solutions and the need for quick action; although this offers satisfactory solutions in the moment, little attention is given to the longer-term impact of the action. We frequently find ourselves taking one step forward toward our goals only to move two steps back when the longer-term impact is experienced (e.g., the extensive impact of the Subprime Mortgage Crisis of 2008 may have been impacted by a short-term perspective on credit and borrowing without importance given to the view to longer-term implications).

Finally, in our discussion of this dilemma it is important to recognize that countries have a varied way of emphasizing past, present, or future. This emphasis influences how next steps are determined and how strong an influence our past experiences have in forecasting the future, or if the future is even considered in responding to the present. Cultures with longer histories (Chinese, Indian, Semitic) take a longer view of time and action. In short-term cultures the memory of past actions is short-lived, but in long-term cultures the past remains present and drives behavior and decisions.

## Time Orientation

Each organization has its own unique time culture and there are many factors that influence this including the marketplace and country of operation. A normal work-week varies across culture. In Hong Kong it is not unusual to have people working daily until 9 or 10 pm at night, while Sunday is sacred time for the family; in London as people rush to catch the train they arrive at work at 9:00 am and are out the door before 6:00 pm, their lives structured by the schedule of public transport. In Malaysia, the workday begins at 9:00 am and ends by 6:00 pm for most managers, who may use lunches and evening hours to build relationships with clients; Friday afternoons are devoted to prayer and extended lunches, with religion taking precedence over work. In Switzerland it is not unusual for a Manager to arrive at her office at 7:00 am, use the first hour for uninterrupted work, and end the day by 4:00 pm, leaving significant time for the pursuit of leisure activities with family and friends.

The time culture of the country and the organization influences the number of hours worked and defines what free time and work-life balance really mean in a cultural context. Work hours are impacted by how truly global an organization is. It has been our experience (and frustration) that work hours are honored primarily at headquarter locations. The former colonialist perspective still influences times for virtual meetings, and it is not unusual for colleagues in locations across the globe to work their local hours and still be available for conferences and meetings during the working hours of HQ time. What this has meant for those working in Asia for East Coast based U.S. corporations is that they find themselves attending conference calls and virtual meetings between 9:00 pm and 1:00 am; for staff of British firms in Asia their day is extended to speak with those in London who schedule meetings only after 9:00 am (so meetings with a manager in Japan begin after 6:00 pm). The greatest challenge is finding a time to meet across the globe with team members from the United States, Europe, the Middle East, Africa, and Asia. Spanning the range of time zones ensures that work is being conducted for someone either before dawn or close to midnight.

*Flex-time* is an approach advocated primarily in Europe and North America. As the name suggests, more flexibility to the work day is built in allowing employees greater freedom in determining the hours that best suit the other demands on their lives. A study was done in Germany to examine the model of flex-time and the influence it had on "trust" between manager and employee. Arrangements were made between employees and their supervisors and colleagues to establish individual working hours and agree on dates and times for completion of assignments.[1] There were clear benefits to having these working arrangements and at the same time there were clear warning signals of the inherent risks if work was not done well.

Flex-time involves an individualistic orientation. For employees the benefits include becoming more autonomous and more personally motivated; as a result their work may be infused with greater levels of innovation. The potential risks of flex-time are that it may cause tension within work teams that have to coordinate the various scheduling needs of the team members, it requires a fine-tuned system of communication, and for some employees the lack of fixed time schedules creates uncertainty and diminishes their effectiveness. Although flex-time has been an option for almost 20 years in the West, the majority of employees continue with the well-established fixed times previously implemented. This offers little opportunity for others desiring schedule flexibility. While many multinationals offer flex-time and virtual work settings in the United States, little of this is reflected in Asia or the Middle East, perhaps because of their focus on the group rather than the individual.

## Time Perspective

Another important result that is being recognized more and more in the global marketplace is how organizations that are socially responsible are furthering local development and sustaining the world. Companies have discovered that these longer-term decisions are enhancing their financial success, are improving the lives of their employees and others within the countries in which they are based, and are responding to the needs to protect and preserve our environment for the future of the planet. Organizations are recognizing their accountability for the impact of their short-term and long-term decisions on the environment far more than ever before and consumers are demanding that organizations incorporate this consciousness into the way they conduct their business.

Short-term focus—like Nike's "just do it"—emphasizes simplicity over complexity and task accomplishment over relationship. There are many who suggest that as our world has become this global village our lives have increased in complexity, and that by focusing on individual aspects and taking rapid action we actually are creating the problems that will be faced by ourselves and others in the near and distant future. Taking a longer-term focus recognizes the need to develop trusting relationships and to study the complexity and systemic nature of situations. Like the Japanese game of "GO" (Chinese game of Wéiqi) it requires a thoughtful plan to accomplish our goals and to succeed.

## PARADOX OF RESPONSE SCENARIO

In the following scenario the elements of time orientation and time perspective influence the interactions between two partners in a global management consulting organization. In this organizational setting, the Partner in Charge (Managing Director) of an office may be on assignment from other countries and be conducting business within different cultures. One of the main criteria for how Managing Directors are selected is the value they can bring to the office in terms of the stage of development of the office (whether it is a start-up or is seasoned), the industry expertise that they bring, and the ability to develop a local team to respond to global and local clients.

### Interaction between Dierk and Kim

Scenario:
Dierk has been a successful Director in the firm for more than 18 years and has served as Managing Director of the firm's Hamburg office. The Seoul office was under the guidance of the Hamburg office, as it is the custom in this firm for more established offices to support offices in newer locations. The Seoul office was established about 10 years ago and enjoyed slow and steady growth from the start. In the past 3 years the growth spurt was significant and the systems in place in the office were deemed insufficient to sustain the growth and to serve their clients successfully.

Offices within the firm serve both local clients, and are instrumental in helping the firm support their global clients, which contribute to a strong part of the firm's success. Therefore, there is a vested interest within the firm to ensure that the Seoul office receives the support it needs to ensure its ability to respond in a timely manner to offices around the globe. Many of the European and American offices have relied on Korea's support for their major clients; however, responses in the past 2 years have not been perceived by European and American offices as either dependable or timely.

Mr. Kim was the acting Managing Director before Dierk arrived. He had been spearheading the office's local growth and responsible for a significant part of its recent expansion. Kim has been with the firm for 9 years and believes he is responsive to the needs of the clients, the office, and the firm in his marketplace.

Kim previously worked with Dierk on a client assignment and was looking forward to working with him again as he knew he could benefit from Dierk's long-term expertise. At the same time he was a little disappointed that he hadn't been made Managing Director considering his successful track record in the office and in the firm thus far. He did not mention this disappointment to anyone.

Dierk arrived and began working under a very tight time frame. Although he still had many important client obligations in Germany he relocated to Seoul and was expected to make an immediate difference. Dierk was looking forward to working with Kim again and gaining his insight for the systemic changes that needed to take place in the office. He planned to split his time between the two offices for the first 5 or 6 months until the current phase of his client work in Germany was completed.

During the first week in the Seoul office Dierk and Kim spent much time together reviewing the state of affairs of the office. During the second week Dierk spent time meeting with other consultants and staff in the office and during the third week he went on some client visits with consultants. The fourth week he was back in Germany.

A month later Dierk returned to Korea. He was feeling good about the office and the changes he was going to lead. In conversations he reviewed these plans with Kim and others, asking for feedback and sharing the timeframe he expected. Everyone seemed to be in agreement and all seemed to be going well.

Another month passed and there didn't seem to be any observable changes taking place. When Dierk questioned Kim about this Kim assured him that the changes were underway and the staff and consultants in the office were on board. Kim reminded Dierk that the group was attending to the growing local client base as well as the global clients. He noted that everyone was committed to furthering the success and growth experienced in the past 3 years. He encouraged Dierk to attend to his client work and not to worry as everything was under control. At the same time, other Directors from around the firm were asking Dierk for progress reports. Based on these conversations Dierk assured them that all was going according to plan. In the meantime, Dierk continued to commute between Germany and Korea completing client work in Germany and managing his relocation to the Seoul office.

The fourth month passed and again Dierk didn't notice any observable changes. He was beginning to show signs of frustration. He challenged Kim and others and held numerous meetings to gather information with the intention of furthering the change process. He was always greeted with agreement and apparent compliance.

Directors from other offices in the firm needing support for their clients from the Seoul office were sharing their frustrations with Dierk noting that there didn't seem to be any change in response time and they needed more support. It was critical for the firm. Dierk began to question the competence of the consultants in the Seoul office and he couldn't understand how they were all agreeing with him and the change initiative, yet no apparent changes were taking place.

When he met with Kim toward the end of the fourth month, Dierk wavered between thinking of the Korean team as either incompetent or resistant to change. The firm needed results and needed them in the immediate timeframe. Dierk was tired of being reassured that the changes were in place when there was no visible difference and the feedback from partners across the globe suggested that the needed support was not forthcoming on a timely basis.

Dierk transferred to the South Korean office with the intent to increase its efficiency and effectiveness and to ensure that it would deliver results according to the established standards and global practice of the firm. There are both implicit and explicit sets of rules and responsibilities for every office as a member of the global alliance. The primary purpose of each office was to serve both global and local clients meeting firm-wide standards.

The Korean market is one of great interest to corporations that are clients of the firm, and these clients expected to have their Korean interests served in the same manner by the firm's office in Seoul as they were served in their home markets. Dierk provided direction to the Seoul office instituting changes that would ensure that they became more responsive to the needs of these global clients. Yet, in conversations and e-mails from directors in various locations across the world Dierk was informed repeatedly that work was still not being delivered according to the time standards he set with the team.

In transition between his former role in Germany and the full relocation to Seoul, Dierk was relying on Kim to ensure that changes were enacted that would bring the response time to standard. When he repeatedly asked Kim and the team to report on the status of changes, he was informed that everything was moving forward and in good order.

Dierk is frustrated with Kim and others in the Seoul office because the verbal messages and actions do not appear to be in sync with one another. Dirk is confused by the situation; he worked with Kim previously on an important client assignment and found him to be a consummate professional and valuable member of the practice.

Kim has been acting Managing Director of the Seoul office for the past 18 months and with the firm for 9 years. He believes he understands the goals of the firm and the relationship of the Seoul office to the rest of the firm. He also believes that he and the Korean team have played a major role in building the Korean business and developing the client base to where it is today. He understands the local clients and has been steadily building a very good rapport with them, which is evidenced in the recent growth.

Kim feels an enormous amount of pressure from Dierk to show results before they can be realistically achieved. Kim balances support to the core Korean clients—Daewoo, Samsung, and Hyundai—who deliver 75% of Korea's annual income with responsiveness to the global work. While he hasn't expressed this directly to Dierk, he has reviewed the financials of the office in detail with him and be-lieves that Dierk should recognize the long-term importance of sus-taining these relationships while building new ones with the local of-fices of global clients.

Kim's previous experience with Dierk was different from their present relationship. In the project their relationship was collegial. He is now experiencing a different side of Dierk and he is not sure what to think. He wishes Dierk would listen to him and trust that he knows what is best in the Korean business environment.

In this scenario we meet two capable people who have been suc-cessful in their own domains and who are becoming increasingly frustrated with each other and less productive in the current situa-tion. Some guiding questions we can ask to better understand the dynamic forces that are creating this scenario are given in Figure 6.1.

---

**FIGURE 6.1**
**Guiding Questions to Understand the Interaction**
**between Dierk and Kim**

- What are Dierk's goals and what is the time frame within which he thinks they can be achieved?
- What are Kim's goals and what is the time frame within which he thinks they can be achieved?
- What is driving the timing of these changes that need to be done in the Seoul office?
- What role does the global firm outside of Seoul play in this situation? What are their expectations?

---

Let's look at these questions and try to understand them in the context of this scenario.

## DIERK'S GOALS

As mentioned earlier, Dierk has been successful in his career as a management consultant and he has been able to strike a successful blend of applying Eurocentric or western management principles to the work he has done with clients around the globe. This is not the first time he has encountered resistance about timing. In the past he has been able to simply push hard enough to drive through what he needed to accomplish within a manageable time frame. In client engagements, he is hired for his expertise, so more often than not clients defer to him and follow his timeline. Because he is a senior partner in the firm his teams complete their work within the time frame he has established.

In his work Dierk expects there will be problems, which is why he is often being called upon. If clients could manage all this on their own they would not be calling on the services of his firm. When projects occasionally hit roadblocks and have been delayed Dierk has been able to manage these slowdowns by working with people within the client team to get things done. Being based in Germany, he has been living and working in a culture surrounded by people who meet established deadlines without question or delay.

The surprise in this situation for Dierk is that Kim as a fellow member of the firm's leadership team is not meeting agreed-upon time frames. He expected Kim to understand the immediate importance of responding to the requests of the firm's global partners within an acceptable period of time. The use of the word "acceptable" is where Dierk made his assumption. He assumed that because the Korean team knew the expectations of the firm, they would adhere to them. By explaining his goals for the office and clarifying the firm's immediate needs, Dierk expected that within 2 to 3 months there would be significant change, just as he would have expected were this the German office.

Another surprise for Dierk was that he thought he knew what to expect. Earlier in his career he had lived in Japan for two years and so he believed he understood the differences between the German office and the Asian offices. As he reflected back on his experience in the Japan office he tried to draw some parallels. He remembered similar frustrations, but that they did not seem to last as long and he was trying to remember why that happened. He recalled that there was a greater presence of consultants from outside Japan and that there were more clients who were subsidiaries of their foreign clients. The more he reflected on these factors, the more he thought they played a role in the current dynamics taking place in the Seoul office. Besides his frustrations he was also disappointed in himself for not making some of these connections sooner.

## KIM'S GOALS

Kim expected that as a long-term member of the firm who had worked in the Korean business environment successfully and had built a strong client base he would be consulted on the nature of the changes to be made in the Seoul office. He believed that his experience would offer insight into how these changes should best be implemented and the time frame within which to make the agreed upon changes.

At the same time he also understood that he was not the senior Director and that he should, therefore, defer to Dierk. He believed he had the cultural authority from which to make useful recommendations, although he hesitated to do so as he did not wish to be perceived as overstepping his boundaries. In addition, he also had a personal relationship with Dierk having previously worked with him.

Kim understood his Korean clients (both local corporations and offices of global enterprises) and knew that in this marketplace they wanted first to build relationships and trust and then ascertain when to engage in the work that needed to be done. Kim and the other consultants in the Seoul office also believed there was an optimal time to make the changes and since timing was so critical rushing to enforce changes too quickly was not always best for long-term success.[2] He was torn between these beliefs concerning what was best in the Korean business milieu and the values of the firm and time pressure being exerted by the firm.

## DRIVING FORCES

The driving forces behind making the changes in the Seoul office were coming from outside Seoul, from the rest of the firm. The firm, primarily considering their immediate short-term needs, needed the Seoul office to respond to their clients more efficiently. They were concerned about the slow pace of the Seoul office. They failed to appreciate or understand the values and focus that the Korean consultants who were acculturated in the Korean tradition brought to the job and failed to understand the importance of keeping the longer-term in focus.

These driving forces centered on competing demands about time and resulted in distress and tension in the office. Kim and the consultants understood the needs of the firm and their Korean clients and thought they were in the best position to interpret both the needs of their Korean clients and the firm. While conceptually this all seemed to make sense, in practice they were hitting walls.

## ROLE OF THE FIRM

The firm is a global network that shares its resources, unique expertise, and approaches around the world; at the same time it operates each office locally. There were many ongoing conversations about the firm's real and perceived value and it was often discussed whether the firm should continue to maintain the Eurocentric behaviors and attitudes that had successfully served them for the past 50 years. The question they were considering was whether they needed to modify their approach to become more attuned to what was taking place as the economic power appeared to be shifting or equalizing between East and West. To what degree should local values be reflected in their practice at each location?

The local application of its approaches, or as mentioned earlier, when practices are tailored to local specifications, also known as "glocalization," is something the firm engages in with its clients. When it comes to practices and interchanges across the firm, however, there is a standard style of communication and standard expectations that are universal, regardless of any potential local variations. This had been considered one of the firm's strengths as it provided a uniformity that expedited delivery of high quality services and facilitated understanding and client satisfaction.

In the case of the Korea office, the firm expected the requested changes to be made in a short period of time. They expected that the consultants to varying degrees were familiar with the practices of the firm and would, therefore, comply with making rapid adjustments. They assumed that the delay in making these changes was due to the consultants in the Seoul office moving at a pace slower than the pace of the consultants in Munich, London, or New York. They also thought that with Dierk's presence, support, and expertise it would just take a short time for the changes to occur.

The Directors in many locations were wondering what the delays were about and why it was taking such a long period of time for them to occur. They continued to question Dierk for clarification. Dierk felt pressure from their questions thinking they were judging him; he felt inadequate because he couldn't respond with useful explanations.

In many situations we are not aware that there may be different ways to understand how time can be framed. We assume that others will share whatever guidelines we use to frame time. We also assume that what we determine to be important and urgent others will classify in the same way. However, even if they do classify the same topics as important they may not act on them in the same time frame because they may address the criteria differently. It is not until we are faced with difference that we come to recognize that our assumptions are not proven, but instead are contradicted. This becomes the paradox we face in the Paradox of Response.

## TIME CONCEPTS

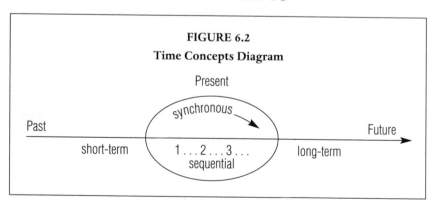

**FIGURE 6.2**

**Time Concepts Diagram**

## Sequential/Synchronous

One way of framing how events take place is by thinking of them as *sequential* or as *synchronous* (Figure 6.2).[3] In framing time as sequential, there is a belief that opportunity comes around once and that this window of opportunity must be seized at that moment. There is also a linear framing of events in which there is a belief that one opportunity comes after the other and that we need to be in a steady state of preparedness so that when an opportunity appears we are ready to embrace it. The sooner and more thoroughly we are prepared, the better it is and the more we can achieve in a shorter period of time. There seems to be a stronger belief in one's own agency in being able to make things happen.

In framing time as synchronous there is a belief that life happens in cycles and what comes around once will come around again. Time flows in a more circular pattern and timing is important. As its label indicates, there is a desired synchronicity with several forces and this synchronicity cannot be rushed or forced by our own efforts alone. There is also deference to forces greater than our own agency and this can also manifest itself in deference to authority.

In the case of Dierk and Kim, Dierk, who was German, was operating more from a sequential orientation in that he had a list of criteria to accomplish and they had to be done in order. This was part of the process of developing smaller offices, and since this approach had been successful in the past, he wanted to continue using the same process. Kim was operating from a more synchronous time orientation in that he knew that eventually there would be opportunities for success as long as he continued to develop and build his client relationships. Relationships are the key to timing and without a solid relationship there could be no good timing. So Kim was more patient, knowing that business development was not tied to the clock, but to a person.

## Monochronic/Polychronic

This is another classification of how time is viewed: *monochronic* time is a linear framing of time with a stronger adherence to clock time, similar to taking a more sequential view of time.[4] Those operating in more monochronic time frames prefer to operate sequentially, focusing on one activity at a time. Time is very important and being on time is critical. There is a literal understanding of time frames and agreements; the assignment is expected on the agreed upon time.

Those with *polychronic* perceptions of time believe that several activities happen simultaneously or overlap and they don't strictly adhere to clock time. An agreed upon time is more of a suggestion of a time frame within which an assignment will be completed. There is an implicit understanding that several activities are taking place simultaneously and while there is a shared intention of completing assignments on time, there is a difference in understanding the meaning of *on time*.

Dierk believed there was an order to how the office needed to be developed and that timing was critical. Certain systems and procedures needed to be put in place before the office could expand. This followed a monochronic pattern of time and reflected the historical orientation of the firm.

Kim, on the other hand, agreed that while the systems and procedures were important, he believed that they could be put in place simultaneous to developing client relationships. He believed in a polychromic sense of time recognizing that even if the systems were underdeveloped as long as the client relationships were strong the clients would understand and all would work out well.

## Short Term/Long Term

In today's global environment with more pressure for ever faster responses and results, we are being pushed into making decisions quickly and to focus on short-term results. It is challenging for us to slow down our process long enough to consider the long-term implications of these quick decisions, because there are many forces that work against this and the momentum is too great. The focus remains on short-term results and less on long-term outcomes and future impact.

As we discussed in Chapter 5 on the Paradox of Action the current business model ensures that we are constantly being evaluated as individuals, as work units, and as organizations; our working relationships and careers are dependent on being able to expedite action. In this environment every operation becomes a transaction with little if any time built in for reflection and planning. When we do consider the importance of planning and put planning sessions in our calendars we frequently find that we neglect the scheduled activity or cancel the meeting. Planning becomes secondary to accomplishing the task at hand.

Long-term framing is more in alignment with synchronous concepts of time. There is a focus on the future and there is an understanding and expectation that there are cycles in the world and in the marketplace and that these affect the work environment. The dilemma between short-term focus and long-term responsiveness requires that challenges are necessary if we are to carefully consider the short-term impact in connection with the long-term implications.

Dierk, and many others in the firm's European and North American locations, supported the short-term goal of immediately getting the office in better working order believing that too much time had already passed. The rest of the firm needed to be able to rely on the Seoul office to support the multinational clients conducting business in Korea. Kim had a longer-term orientation; he knew that building trust was the glue that would enable them to continue to develop good relationships with both local and multinational clients from other offices and that this would secure their success in South Korea. It was not that he did not understand the sense of urgency Dierk and others in the firm were experiencing, but knowing the culture he focused on what was needed for longer-term sustainable business success.

## Past, Present, Future

Time orientations may be classified as *past, present,* and *future.*[5] A focus on the past shows the value of continuing time-honored traditions and moving forward with what went before. Change is not encouraged because there is a belief that what has worked well in the past will continue to be effective. This differs from a focus on the present, which shows a stronger orientation toward short-term, immediate gains. The here and now are most critical. In a future orientation, people and organizations work to fulfill long-term goals even if it means sacrificing short-term gains. The reason this framing of time is important is that it influences how the organization's goals are structured, how the workflow is decided, and what the expected output will be. It influences how requests will be responded to and how demands will be managed.

In the case of Dierk and Kim, Dierk was acting from a present tense framing of the situation. As the Managing Director he was accountable for the immediate results from the Seoul office; although he knew the importance of client relationships, he was not letting that drive his actions and expectations. Kim, on the other hand, focused on preparing for the future; in terms of client relationships his emphasis was on developing future benefits, while respecting the past in the form of tradition. He was willing to forego immediate gains, even though he was being pressured by his firm to emphasize these. While this may have cost him his role as Managing Director, in terms of what was best for the firm he believed that continuing to prepare for the future would work to everyone's advantage; the firm simply needed to wait and trust the process

## UNINTENDED CONSEQUENCES

In any time orientation we take we need to understand that there are consequences. If we take a short-term perspective and take advantage of short-term gains, we may be doing this at the expense of preparing for longer-term sustainability. If we follow a synchronous flow of time we may be juggling too many balls in the air at one time and not complete any one effort in a timely manner. Likewise, if we follow a sequential orientation to time we may thoroughly complete one activity at the expense of forfeiting others because we were not able to entertain other possibilities.

In maintaining systems that have been effective and an orientation to the past, we may be missing opportunities to change and develop for the future. If we maintain the present orientation we may be unable to sustain our efforts. If we maintain a future orientation we may lose too many valuable resources including people in the process.

## SUSTAINABILITY

One area that has been drawing significant attention in recent years is environmental sustainability and the role and responsibility of organizations.[6] We are including it in this section addressing time orientation because it involves both immediate short-term results with built-in long-term viability measures. There is a leaning toward a synchronous rather than a sequential orientation toward time, as there is an understanding that what is done today will impact us in the future. There is a focus on present tense actions reaping present and future tense results.

This consciousness has been referred to as *Corporate Social Responsibility* (CSR), and while the term has various definitions, its main characteristics include the following: enterprises behave ethically and are socially responsible, they participate in the economic and social development of their employees and their families, they positively contribute to the local communities within which they operate, and they go beyond policies and procedures and have full top management support for these efforts.[7]

Because there are many different ways of interpreting CSR best practice and varying ways of enforcing it, including a predominance of self-monitoring, organizations will benefit from more uniform agreement on what needs to be done, how it should be done, and how to measure the progress of these efforts. There are economic drivers, such as risk assessment, customer pressure, investor pressure, and business partner pressures; political drivers, such as regulatory compliance, licensing to operate, and improved standing with governments; and social drivers, such as local community pressure, NGO and CSO pressure, and research findings.[8]

Corporations are acting in more responsible ways on a global level as citizens of the world. One way of defining corporate citizenship is "the business strategy that shapes the values underpinning a company's mission and the choices made each day by its executives, managers and employees as they engage with society."[9] The four core principles of corporate citizenship identified are to minimize harm to stakeholders, the environment, and others; to maximize the benefits to the corporation as well as to stakeholders beyond the organization; to be accountable to key stakeholders by acting with honesty and by building trusting relationships; and to support strong financial results, which includes providing profits for stakeholders.

One example of an environmental nonprofit NGO is Earthwatch, whose mission is to "promote the understanding and action necessary for a sustainable environment. As part of this mission, it is important that Earthwatch manages the environmental and social impacts of its activities, and that Earthwatch acts as a role model for other organizations in terms of sustainable office practices and policies."[10] Earthwatch has an active social responsibility arm and it partners with organizations around the globe; this enables these organizations to better understand the environment and the impact their decisions and actions have both short term and long term. It is a partnership of science and business and to date there are at least 50,000 partnerships between Earthwatch and global organizations.

Global organizations are citizens of the world as they think globally and act locally, and local is any place in the world. Advanced communication, especially electronic with the advent of the internet, promotes closeness. Global organizations in the world of today are under closer scrutiny than ever before and actions that will bear results in the present and in the future will be noticed.[11]

## DEVELOPING A BROADER
## SENSE OF TIME

We suggest that you use Figure 6.3 to assist you as you try to frame the short-term and long-term impact of decisions you are making. It can be used as a conversational tool for yourself or amongst your team or in any interaction in which decisions need to be made and time is an important factor.

**FIGURE 6.3**
**Time Impact Chart**

Past (traditions)

Present (current state)

Future (implications)

Short-term (immediate impact)

Long-term (future impact)

Sequential (linear order)

Synchronous (parallel order)

# 7 | EMBRACING THE PARADOXES

*If you are planning for a year, sow rice;*
*if you are planning for a decade, plant trees*
*if you are planning for a lifetime, educate people.*

—CHINESE PROVERB

We really do live in a global village; we are connected through time and space with all parts of the world everyday and in every way. Our colleagues, team members, customers, and stakeholders are strewn across the globe, yet communication is so easy, a call, an e-mail to our Blackberry™ or iPhone™, an SMS to our phone, a planning session on a "wiki," or a note on our wall in Facebook creates a sense of familiarity and ease that is deceptive. It seems that they are just around the corner.

If we travel to foreign lands to live and work, we are working with those from other cultures. No matter what our position is, it behooves us to remember that it is we who are guests. It is not that they don't speak our language, but frequently transnational leaders don't speak theirs. We have created an exciting life that offers endless opportunities for learning and broadening our understanding of what is "usual." Within the borders of our country, we are as likely to find that our peers who are born or educated in other cultures bring different views, ways of communicating and present ways for us to be influenced by this. As we open ourselves to the differences that surround us, we have the chance to reframe our understanding

American Management Association
www.amanet.org

of the impact and value of assertiveness, harmony, accomplishment, loyalty, conflict, and cooperation.

Through the lens of difference we come to know how to communicate respectfully with others, not expecting them to be like us, but honoring them for being who they are. We have much to learn about each other and from each other. Our first step in the journey as a transnational leader is to learn about ourselves and to experience ourselves as others do.

It is interesting that as we work across borders and boundaries, we are always in a position to reflect and learn from our experiences. Some days, when we are working with those from other cultures, it seems that the paradoxes have disappeared, and just as we start to feel that we understand and are understood, we have a conversation that reminds us that there is still so much that we simply don't know about ourselves and others. That is the magic of transnational leadership; it's a life-long learning opportunity for those who embrace it!

In each of the preceding chapters we introduced you to some of the significant paradoxes facing leaders today. We believe that to be effective in our world all leaders need to frame their leadership as *transnational* because cultural diversity is ever present and becoming more the norm than the exception to the rule. The Chinese move to Japan to take professional jobs, Indians and Malaysian relocate to Singapore, Eastern Europeans settle across Western Europe seeking and securing a place in these societies, and the United States, Australia, and Canada use web advertising to solicit new citizens from those across the globe. To this is added the virtual teams drawn from across the world, the global partnerships and subsidiaries that form "globally integrated enterprises," and the accessibility that technology provides. We are all indeed *transnational leaders.*

Transnational leaders embrace the diversity of thought and behavior present within and surrounding their organizations. Established ways of interacting and conducting the day-to-day operations within the organization are likely to be transformed by the diverse views and practices that are present. This diversity and recognition of a broadening economy require us to rethink our vision, strategy, and goals that need to be established before an organization can set its direction.

When these varied points of view are synthesized constructively we gain access to a rich organizational culture that is mindful, respectful, and representative of the world within which it operates. When diverse opinions are valued and ways of working collaboratively are established, then increased innovation is freed, coordination flourishes, and profitability grows. In this transnational setting everyone benefits.

## THE PARADOX OF KNOWING

In the traditional framing of leadership we think of it as the role of a person who leads others. We believe that leadership begins with the self; as "personal leaders" we lead ourselves everyday recognizing our impact on those around us. In the *paradox of knowing* we demonstrated that to be effective we must first know ourselves. There are many ways in which we can learn about ourselves and we describe knowing ourselves in relation to others.

At the core of all our interpersonal transactions are the values, beliefs, and behaviors we bring that have been culturally developed. We are often unaware of the cultural influences, assumptions, and beliefs we bring to all our relationships. Our experiences are both similar to and different from those with whom we interact and build relationships.

Increasing emphasis on results demands better understanding if we are to work effectively together. We know that when this understanding is absent or underdeveloped, misunderstanding and conflict ensue, negatively impacting interpersonal relationships. This is why it is so critical for us to know who we are and the impact we have on others. Leadership is about impacting others. As leaders we are charged with the responsibility of bringing out the best in those we lead. The more aware we are of the impact we have the more we can tailor our interactions and build positive relationships with others.

## THE PARADOX OF FOCUS

The *paradox of focus* addresses the level at which we are motivated to make decisions and act. Do we move forward considering our own needs? Do we move forward considering the needs of the group to which we belong? Or do we move forward with some creative blend of the two? It is not as clear-cut as it may seem. Traditionally, when there was less interaction with those who were different it was easier to believe that everyone was driven toward the same goals and sought the same accomplishments. We were surrounded by similarity and could balance our need for conformity or individuation and more easily rationalize our obligations.

Today it is more complex because we are working in groups in which there is an array of focus points at times competing with one another. Each of us may feel the tension of the struggle as we are pulled one way or the other and our sense of obligation (to us or to others) becomes more of a question than a foregone conclusion. Today we have a choice, whereas in the past it was an expectation. And now the expectations of the choices we anticipate others will make can add another factor to the complexity. While dilemmas create tension, if we honor them for the gifts of new perspectives, then creative energy is freed as we learn to pay attention to individual and group needs at the same time.

## THE PARADOX OF COMMUNICATION

All of this is either facilitated or blocked by our communication. More than ever before we need to communicate on a regular basis across difference. The demand for expediency adds another layer and is a source of pressure. In the *paradox of communication* we address the degree to which we need to be direct in how we speak with others. There are occasions in which we need to soften our message, while at other times we need to cut to the chase, so to speak. Indirect communication can be considered polite or deceptive and direct communication can be refreshing or rude, all depending on who is in the conversation, their practices, and their expectations.

We've mentioned the presence of expediency in the world within which we work and this prompts many of us to want to expedite the decision-making process. Discussions are geared to making quicker decisions as it calls upon us to present our views in a way that is convincing, assertive, and, on occasion, argumentative. The more we act on this efficiency model the more we may lose opportunities for fuller exploration and innovation. Dialogue is a form of communication more conducive to this process of inquiry and works well with diverse groups of people when there is trust and support. It also helps to foster trust and support because of the very nature of how inclusive dialogue is designed to be. The main point here is to have a repertoire of approaches in communication and select the one(s) that is most suitable at the time. One challenge is that we do not always select the type of communication approach that best matches our immediate needs.

# THE PARADOX OF ACTION

This rushing around and giving in to expediency causes us to overly rely on it, as it becomes the normal way of doing business. At the end of each day we may ask ourselves, "What have I done today and how did I add value?" We no longer have the time to slow down and reflect on what we are doing. In the *paradox of action* we highlight the tension we experience between doing and being. How can we just "be" when we are always compelled to "do"? We believe in and advocate slowing our acting down, so we can take the time to reflect and arrive at a better, more thoughtful action that cannot be performed if we are always on the move.

In yoga there are poses we can do to increase energy, flexibility, and strength and to massage our organs. One important aspect of yoga is to periodically move into certain poses of pure relaxation; this allows the benefits of previous poses to sink in and take hold. There is a cycle of doing and then being that allows each to reinforce and support the other. The same can be said for allowing time to engage in reflective practices so that the benefits of what we do can sink in and take hold.[1] These practices also prepare us for the next set of actions we need to take. This reflective practice provides insights that make us more mindful and help us make more thoughtful choices and decisions.

American Management Association
www.amanet.org

## THE PARADOX OF RESPONSE

We've spoken often about the concept of time and the fact that it is practiced in a wide variety of ways. In the business world there is a growing focus on expediency, but that does not come easily for many. And there is value in slowing down the process to consider long-term implications and not just short-term action. The *paradox of response* addresses the time orientation we bring with us to our interactions with others. If my focus is on the here and now and yours is on the future or the past, we are going to be driven by different sets of motivating factors in the way we make decisions and how we act on them. These different approaches may easily cause friction and conflict. One person may feel delayed by a colleague not focusing on problems that he believes deserve immediate action, another may feel unappreciated for the valuable work delivered in a tried and true way, and a third may be unwilling to succumb to a cry of urgency where none exists. The key is to recognize that there is value in each time process. Those who focus on the past ensure that we continue our best practice, those who focus on the present are forever coming up with new ways and approaches that ensure innovation, and those who look to the future ensure sustainability.

The focus on seeking either short-term solutions or long-term impact for sustainability is a driving force in how we make decisions. The expediency that drives us all to expect and produce immediate results influences us to seek short-term solutions, which may or may not be sustainable over time. Because of this we don't have the time to thoroughly examine the situation at hand

This can also be an addictive way to function. There is a certain adrenaline rush that comes with acting on what we perceive to be urgent. It provides a false sense of importance and errors may be made when we act in haste. It is the equivalent of placing Band-Aids™ on broken systems without the benefit of long-term remedy and care.

## DEVELOPING TRANSNATIONAL LEADERS

We are all proficient in managing these paradoxes to one degree or another depending on the situation and the others who are involved with us. The more aware we become of these factors, the more attention we pay to them and the greater the opportunity to develop our skills. Some of you are responsible for developing other people and we would like to share some thoughts on how to assemble a program or workshop that will train leaders to become more adept at leading transnationally.

We believe that for optimum results and impact support from the organization is needed for this type of work and development; this allows it to take hold in its infancy stages and really be a systemic change. Individual leaders can still move forward in their own personal leadership development by adapting some of the recommendations for each paradox. It is easier, smoother, and more thorough if these changes are done holistically rather than piecemeal. It is also beneficial when done in a group so that a built-in support system is created. When a critical mass is developed within the organization a tipping point[2] is created, which makes it easier for those developing their skills as transnational leaders. Until and even after this type of behavior and belief system becomes the norm, creating a support system with other like-minded folk creates support for those developing their transnational leader skills.

In addition to the developmental aspect of transnational leadership, it is useful for organizations to look at their other business practices to identify how they are addressing these diverse needs. The human resource (HR) group can look at hiring and development practices to ensure that the ways in which they are hiring, developing, and promoting their staff and management are in line with the increasingly diverse compositional needs of the organization. The HR group can also compare the distribution of the diverse characteristics of their staff and management to assess whether it is representational of where the organization operates around the world, including which populations they are serving. It is also a reality check on how well the organization is taking into consideration the markets in which they have a presence or want to have a successful presence.

# EIGHT WORKSHOP DESIGN CONSIDERATIONS

In designing workshops we take into consideration certain underlying principles, such as the different learning needs and objectives of the participants with whom we are working. The first step is to do an assessment of the purpose of the workshop and the desired outcomes of the participants. We begin assessing their learning needs by considering basic principles of adult learners that are critical for ensuring the program is a success, however success is designed and measured.[3] We also use Kolb's learning styles as a guide for ensuring that the ways in which we address the paradoxes incorporate different modes of learning to address different learning styles.[4]

- Identify current awareness, skills, and abilities
- Create situations for the participants to experience the paradoxes
- Have participants refer to their original assessment to compare it to their experience
- Debrief the participants using the five paradox guidelines
- Provide times for praxis, doing, and reflecting
- Include activities to develop awareness, knowledge, and skills for each paradox and how they interact with one another
- Provide exercises so that participants can directly connect this learning with an application back in the workplace
- Provide opportunities for praxis: doing and reflection

It is important to *identify the current awareness, skills, and abilities* of the participants in any program. This allows the participants to determine their current status so they can more readily identify their developmental targets. There is a benefit from a design point of view of having all the participants evaluated against a standard measure. There are numerous ways to do this. One way is to conduct a survey with the questions targeted at the five paradoxes to be covered in the workshop.[5]

This is useful information for the program designer. Activities can be tailored to address the distribution of the participants within the workshop. The more diverse the composition of the group, the more they can experience the measures of the five paradoxes. This is so because it gives the participants the opportunity to interact with others actually holding and living the different extremes of the paradoxes, rather than simply being told about them.

The next step is to *introduce an activity or simulation* that will provide opportunities for the participants to actually experience the paradoxes. There are different levels of learning, and for some, actually feeling the tension and dilemma of operating within these paradoxes at a gut level is more powerful than simply engaging them on a conceptual level. Case studies, simulations, enacting scenes from movies or plays, and other techniques are used alone or in combination. In these activities participants are encouraged to act as they would typically react in a real-life situation. They are encouraged not to play a role because that will distance themselves from the feeling, experience, and potential learning.

After they comment on their experience in the simulation or activity, have them *refer back to their survey results to compare their reactions to the experience* with it. Ask them to look for patterns of consistency that determine how closely the results match the experience and also to look for contradictions. This is all useful information for self-awareness and development. There is no right or wrong information, only information that will guide us in learning more about ourselves. This enables the participants to be more self-motivated and to seek ways in which they can relieve the tensions they are experiencing and thereby become more effective transnational leaders.

With the experience as a common reference point we can now *introduce the five paradoxes,* their characteristics, and their impact. The participants have their visceral encounter with the paradoxes through the simulation or activity; this provides them with a real experience that aids in understanding the paradoxes from more than a conceptual point of view. It is useful to discuss the experiences of the participants, such as what came easy and what was a struggle; this will enable them to connect the conceptual learning with the experiential learning, resulting in a fuller more robust learning experience. This addresses the different learning styles as defined by Kolb, mentioned earlier.

It is important that participants be provided with *opportunities to reflect and engage in praxis, doing, and reflecting,* throughout the workshop. This allows them to understand the paradoxes involved, their behavior, and the reactions of others to them on an individual basis, and to see how this aligns with their desired outcomes. The chance to reflect deepens the learning experience and allows the pace to be slowed down; this allows the participants to absorb more information that they can then use in subsequent activities. It supports the paradox of action principles of doing and being.

Now that the participants have obtained insight into their own placement on the continuums of the five paradoxes, had a simulated experience of how these paradoxes play out in real interactions, and learned more about the characteristics of each paradox, it is time to *develop skills in how to successfully address the paradoxes.* There are numerous ways to do this including exploring cases studies, role-plays, and communication techniques. On a conceptual level it is easy to understand the characteristics of each paradox. The behavioral level is more challenging for here it is necessary to internalize the conceptual understanding and act on it accordingly.

For the purpose of understanding we take the paradoxes apart and analyze them one by one. In reality, doing this is not so clear-cut as the paradoxes interact with one another for a more complex rendering. How this plays out also needs to be explored so that each paradox is correctly identified and not confused with any other. This is important because there is a chance that misunderstanding will cause us to select behaviors that will not be as effective as those that would be chosen with a more accurate connection to the correct paradox.

After all this exploration the participants will need to make some deliberate connections between what they have learned about themselves and the paradoxes so that they can *transfer this learning back to the workplace.* The more specific the participants can be about how they will apply this new learning, the greater the chance that they will actually apply it. Creating a support network for the participants will enable them to carry out their plans of action. This can be created by having the participants remain in contact with one another for continued support and reinforcement. Supports can be put in place in the work environment so that colleagues and more senior management can provide continued learning opportunities, coaching, and feedback, enabling the participants to continue building their skills on this journey.

We believe that transformative learning theory provides a foundation for the work that we do. Implicit in the above description are the principals of transformative learning. In Appendix 2 we offer further insight on the application of transformative learning in developing transnational leaders.

# APPENDIX 1
# TOOLS

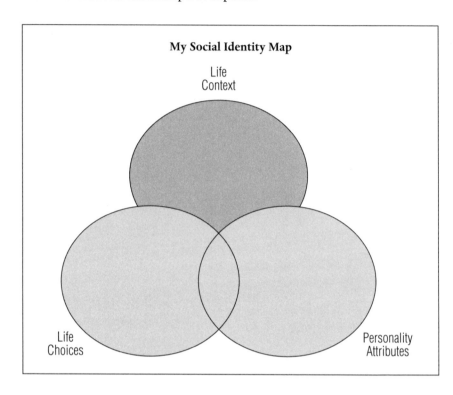

**My Social Identity Map**

Life
Context

Life
Choices

Personality
Attributes

**Values Chart**

| | | |
|---|---|---|
| Abundance | Awareness | Compassion |
| Acceptance | Balance | Completion |
| Accessibility | Being the best | Conformity |
| Accomplishment | Belonging | Connection |
| Accuracy | Boldness | Consistency |
| Achievement | Brilliance | Contribution |
| Acknowledgement | Calmness | Control |
| Adaptability | Camaraderie | Conviction |
| Affection | Capability | Cooperation |
| Agility | Certainty | Courage |
| Anticipation | Challenge | Courtesy |
| Appreciation | Clarity | Creativity |
| Approachability | Clear-mindedness | Credibility |
| Assertiveness | Cleverness | Daring |
| Attentiveness | Comfort | Decisiveness |
| Availability | Commitment | Deference |

| | | |
|---|---|---|
| Dependability | Frugality | Persuasiveness |
| Determination | Generosity | Power |
| Dignity | Gratitude | Practicality |
| Directness | Growth | Pragmatism |
| Discipline | Happiness | Preparedness |
| Discovery | Harmony | Presence |
| Diversity | Helpfulness | Privacy |
| Drive | Honesty | Perfection |
| Dynamism | Hopefulness | Professionalism |
| Eagerness | Humility | Reasonableness |
| Economy | Humor | Recognition |
| Education | Imagination | Reflection |
| Effectiveness | Impact | Reliability |
| Efficiency | Impartiality | Resilience |
| Empathy | Inquisitiveness | Resourcefulness |
| Encouragement | Insightfulness | Professionalism |
| Endurance | Inspiration | Reasonableness |
| Energy | Integrity | Recognition |
| Enjoyment | Intelligence | Reflection |
| Enthusiasm | Intensity | Reliability |
| Excellence | Intuitiveness | Resilience |
| Expediency | Inventiveness | Resourcefulness |
| Experience | Keenness | Sacrifice |
| Fairness | Kindness | Self-control |
| Family | Knowledge | Selflessness |
| Financial freedom | Leadership | Self-reliance |
| Firmness | Learning | Sensitivity |
| Fitness | Liberty | Significance |
| Flexibility | Logic | Sincerity |
| Focus | Love | Spontaneity |
| Fortitude | Loyalty | Stability |
| Frankness | Make a difference | Support |
| Freedom | Mastery | Teamwork |
| Friendliness | Mellowness | Thoroughness |
| Frugality | Mindfulness | Timeliness |
| Fun | Obedience | Trustworthiness |
| Firmness | Open-mindedness | Uniqueness |
| Fitness | Openness | Unity |
| Flexibility | Optimism | Usefulness |
| Focus | Originality | Utility |
| Fortitude | Passion | Valor |
| Frankness | Peace | Variety |
| Freedom | Perfection | Warmth |
| Friendliness | Persistence | Wittiness |

**Values Chart Worksheet**

| Ten values most important | My definition of this value |
| --- | --- |
| 1. _____ | _____ |
| 2. _____ | _____ |
| 3. _____ | _____ |
| 4. _____ | _____ |
| 5. _____ | _____ |
| 6. _____ | _____ |
| 7. _____ | _____ |
| 8. _____ | _____ |
| 9. _____ | _____ |
| 10. _____ | _____ |

**Values and Their Impact on Me**

| Value | How it shapes your life and impacts your decisions and choices |
| --- | --- |
| 1. _____ | _____ |
| 2. _____ | _____ |
| 3. _____ | _____ |

## Reflection on Social Identity and Values

Individual Reflection: Social Identity and values

- Reflecting on your social identity and values how do they influence your life choices?
- How do they impact upon your relationships with others?
- How do they enhance and limit the effectiveness of your interactions with those from other cultures?
- How are they evident in your behavior as a leader?

## Assessing the Paradox of Focus

| Characteristic | Criteria—define for each characteristic | High | Medium | Low |
|---|---|---|---|---|
| Independence in working style. | Working Style (define) | | | |
| Interdependence in working style. | Working Style | | | |
| Open communication in group. | Communication | | | |
| Open disagreement or conflict. | Conflict | | | |
| Time and efficiency are a priority | Time | | | |
| Care taken to not offend any group member | Interpersonal Dynamics | | | |
| Expedient decisions reached | Decision-making | | | |
| Assuring consensus for decisions. | Decision-making | | | |
| Praise given to individual accomplishments. | Recognition | | | |
| Praise given to group accomplishments | Recognition | | | |

**Planning Your Strategy for the Paradox of Focus**

| Criteria | Strategic action steps: |
| --- | --- |
| Working style | _____ |
| | _____ |
| Communication | _____ |
| | _____ |
| Conflict management | _____ |
| | _____ |
| Interpersonal dynamics | _____ |
| | _____ |
| Decision making | _____ |
| | _____ |
| Reward or recognition | _____ |
| | _____ |

---

**"LIVE" Dialogue**

# L ? V <3

- *Listening* with openness to understand
- *Inquiry* with curiosity to learn
- *Voicing* our thoughts and feelings to be heard
- *Empathy* with respectful understanding of others

## Worksheet for Transnational Communication

| Characteristic | Notes |
|---|---|
| Direct / Indirect ←——————→ | |
| Discussion / Dialogue ←——————→ | |
| Linear / Circular - ←——————→ | |
| **L (listening)** What do I need to listen for? What do I need to do to show I am listening? How can I make sure I am being listened to? | |
| **? (inquiry)** What do I need to know? How shall I frame my questions? How can I ensure my questions are received openly? | |
| **V (voice)** What do I need to do to ensure I allow the other person to have voice? What do I need to do to ensure I have voice? | |
| **<3 (empathy)** what do I need to be empathic about? How can I show empathy? | |

**Reflection Process Chart**

Group

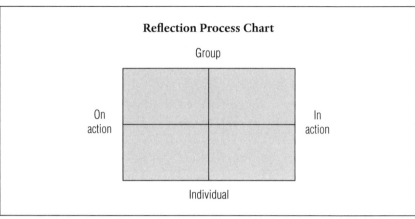

On
action

In
action

Individual

**Quadrants of Reflection Chart with Guiding Questions**

GROUP

|  |  |
|---|---|
| 1. What worked well and how did we benefit? | 1. What is working well and how are we benefiting? |
| 2. What assumptions did we make? | 2. What assumptions are we making? |
| 3. What can we do differently? | 3. What can we do differently? |
| 4. What challenges did we face? | 4. What challenges are we facing? |
| 5. What did we do to overcome them? | 5. What are we doing to overcome them? |

ON
ACTION

IN
ACTION

|  |  |
|---|---|
| 1. What worked well and how did I benefit? | 1. What is working well and how am I benefiting? |
| 2. What assumptions did I make? | 2. What assumptions am I making? |
| 3. What can I do differently? | 3. What can I do differently? |
| 4. What challenges did I face? | 4. What challenges am I facing? |
| 5. What did I do to overcome them? | 5. What am I doing to overcome them? |

INDIVIDUAL

**Suggested Tips**

- Carry the reflective questions around with you so that practicing them becomes a habit.

- Build in time for individual and group reflection as part of group work, including team meetings.

- Practice doing reflection "on action" with the goal of integrating this real time to become "in action" as well.

- Examine your assumptions to better understand why you operate the way you do and to attain deeper self-awareness.

- Practice freeze framing and taking a meta-view to hone your observational skills.

- Consider unintended consequences that may arise from your actions, especially when the intent and impact are not in alignment.

## Time Impact Chart

| | |
|---|---|
| Past (traditions) | |
| Present (current state) | |
| Future (implications) | |
| Short-term (immediate impact) | |
| Long-term (future impact) | |
| Sequential (linear order) | |
| Synchronous (parallel order) | |

# APPENDIX 2
## TRANSFORMATIVE LEARNING IN HUMAN RESOURCE DEVELOPMENT AND SUCCESSES IN PRACTITIONER APPLICATIONS: CONFLICT MANAGEMENT AND LEADERSHIP DEVELOPMENT

## TRANSFORMATIVE LEARNING PRACTITIONER APPLICATIONS

In *Advances in Developing Human Resources* (2004) Brooks indicates that transformative learning is a viable theory and research approach for developing human resources.[1] She notes that transformative learning provides a basis for developing people in whom "a change in level of conscious awareness is appropriate such as managing across national boundaries, learning to be part of a diverse workforce, adjusting to mergers and acquisitions, dealing with complexity, motivating others, and making sense of work in an era of downsizing, involuntary reassignments and changes in the psychological work contract" (Brooks, 2004, p. 220). There are those who challenge Brooks' assertion, questioning whether experiences can be structured to be transformative. As practitioners who have consciously designed transformative learning interventions to develop managers, our experience leads us to support Brooks' assertion. In this appendix we provide an overview of our experience with the application of transformative learning theory in human resource development.

We will first operationalize transformative learning theory identifying six dynamics that provide a context for the design of specific interventions. We then provide specific applications. What makes our experience unique is that we have applied transformative learning in both North American and global (Asian, African, and Middle Eastern) contexts. We believe that human resource development programs designed intentionally to incorporate the transformative learning process foster both individual and organizational transformations.

## THE DYNAMICS OF
## TRANSFORMATIVE LEARNING

Over the last quarter of the twentieth century transformative learning has developed into the leading adult learning theory. Transformative learning offers a multifaceted process through which learners identify, deconstruct, and give new meaning to their experience. The current conceptualization of transformative learning refers to a process

> By which we transform our taken-for-granted frames of reference (meaning perspectives, habits of mind, mind-sets) to make them more inclusive, discriminating, open, emotionally capable of change, and reflective so that they may generate beliefs and opinions that will prove more true or justified to guide action. (Mezirow, 2000, p. 7)

Transformative learning theory incorporates a constructivist focus on individual development and rational thought and reflection, while bringing to the fore the importance of cultural context, group learning, and discourse (Mezirow, 1991; Cranton, 1994). It suggests a learning process for developing socially responsible, clear-thinking decision makers who use self understanding and critical reflection to challenge assumptions and to increase their understanding of complex situations, question conformity, embrace change, and align their actions for the betterment of society (Brookfield, 1987; Marsick, 1990; Mezirow, 1990, 2000; Dirkx, 1997; Kasl & Yorks, 2002). Through the use of dialogue in conversation and the conscious development of mutuality, participants in a transformative learning process gain awareness of their personal beliefs, values, and feelings. By engaging others in this learning they gain an appreciation of a wide range of beliefs, values, and feelings, recognizing that perceptions and actions are the result of how people see the world. Transformative learning establishes the importance of reflection in the workplace.

> Workplaces are not typically associated with reflection. . . . Yet paradoxically, reflection is becoming more part of the lifeblood of organizations in today's turbulent economic environment. . . . Frequently trained to implement policies rationally, managers are being called upon to make subjective judgments, take risks, and question the assumptions on which they have operated. (Marsick, 1990, p. 23)

Transformative learning provides a theory of adult learning for developing leaders and associates who are willing to challenge the status quo and actively ask, as Argyris (1993) suggests, "Are we doing the right thing" and "Why are we doing this." It provides learning that fosters organizationally and socially responsible decision making and culture change.

Taylor (2000, 2003) offers an extensive review of transformative learning theory research identifying several themes that arise naturally from the empirical perspective. As he notes, "Found essential to making meaning is understanding of one's frame of reference, the role of the disorienting dilemma, critical reflection, dialogue with others, and conditions that foster transformative learning to name a few" (Taylor, 2000, p. 287). Building on Taylor's analytical reviews and conducting a thorough review of this family of theory, research, and practice we have identified six dynamics of transformative learning to make this theory operational for human resource development practitioners (Geller, 2004)

Identifying our current frames of reference and deconstructing them through self-reflection is the first dynamic action in the transformative learning process. Gaining awareness of familial, cultural, and stereotypic beliefs influences the way people in work settings experience the self, others, and events. Critical reflection is the second dynamic. It provides the means for identifying and challenging assumptions and exploring and imagining alternatives. Thinking critically may result in innovative ways of engaging with the world as an individual comes to learn that "There are no fixed truths or totally definitive knowledge" (Mezirow, 2000, p. 3). Brookfield (1987) defines critical thinking as a productive and positive contextual activity, triggered by both positive and negative events, that incorporates the emotive and rational. As he notes, "When we become critical thinkers . . . we become skeptical of quick-fix solutions, of single answers to problems, and of claims to universal truth. In this process the person develops alternative ways of looking at and behaving in the world" (p. ix).

Praxis, reflection on action, becomes the third dynamic of transformative learning. Praxis is the process of learning through the reconstruction of experience. It encapsulates questioning the problem, which enables us to consider the situation in a new way. When action and reflection are integrated, actions are considered not in light of *how do we do this, but rather in terms of what do we believe taking this action will do; why are we doing this; what don't we know about taking this action; and what alternatives are there that we still have to consider?* Praxis allows action to be delayed, providing time to consider the implications and long-term impact of the action, creating a fuller understanding of what is proposed, and providing time to consider other possible alternatives.

The fourth and fifth dynamics of transformational learning—dialogue and empathy—have their basis in reflective discourse. Dialogue involves "the assessment of beliefs, feelings and . . . [it] involves an intrapersonal process, drawing on the information one has about the speaker . . . [it] also involves an interpersonal dimension, using feedback to adapt messages to the other's perspective" (Mezirow, 2003, pp. 59–60). Empathy is the act of creating understanding among a group through the creation of a horizontal relationship based on mutual trust and solidarity (Freire, 1970).

> The sixth and final dynamic of transformative learning is intercultural appreciation. Transformative learning is based in the contextual understanding of the self and the other. It presents a learning process that allows for the intrapersonal and interpersonal understanding of frames of reference. And frames of reference are initially developed

through socio-cultural beliefs, values and perspectives acquired in our family of origin, cultural assimilation, and stereotypic representations within our society. This final dynamic offered by transformative learning allows for the exploration of cultural, language and style differences. In this process of exploring frames of reference, people develop an understanding and appreciation of difference. Through discourse and dialogue they can inquire into meanings behind both linear and contextual representations. Transformative learning through its interwoven dynamics—self-reflection, critical thinking, praxis, empathy, dialogue and intercultural appreciation—offers a learning process that serves as a structural basis for the development of human resource development programs that support personal and organizational transformations.

## TRANSFORMATIVE LEARNING IN PRACTICE

There is a debate ongoing in the field of transformative learning about whether we can structure an experience so that it is transformative for people. Our belief is that we can set up the environment both in terms of the structure of the workshop as well as the processes used to encourage transformative learning experiences. The use of dialogue, feedback, role playing, and storytelling creates relationships and dynamics that foster a broadened perspective and the occurrence of transformative experiences.

What does the transformative learning process incorporate? Learners in the transformative learning process primarily learn from each other. The "trainer" becomes a "facilitator of reasoning in a learning situation and a cultural activist fostering the social, economic, and political conditions required for fuller, freer participation in critical reflection and discourse" (Mezirow, 2003, p. 63). The transformative learning methodology includes the use of critical incidents, metaphors from literature, music, and art, appreciative inquiry, dialogue, and group participation in social action (Cranton, 1994; Mezirow, 1997; Taylor, 2000). The learning process occurs through intentional effort and is designed to "foster critically reflective thought, imaginative problem posing, and discourse that is learner centered, participatory and interactive. . . .

Instructional materials reflect real-life experiences. . . . Learning contracts, group projects, role play, case studies, and simulations are all methods associated with transformative education" (Mezirow, 1997, p. 11).

Transformative learning offers a reflective and discursive learning process that serves to illuminate beliefs, values, and assumptions for the self and the other; it broadens the understanding that truth is not an absolute, but is contextually influenced and personally constructed; it engages people in the communal process of dialogue; and it reveals the higher purpose against which decisions are assessed and their implications understood (Mezirow 1990, 1991, 2000; Cranton, 1994).

## SUCCESSES IN SCHOLARLY PRACTITIONER APPLICATIONS: CONFLICT MANAGEMENT

When people in conflict take action to resolve it, they may choose from a number of approaches. The word conflict as used here can be defined as "the experience of incompatible activities" (Coleman, 2003). "An incompatible activity prevents, obstructs, interferes, injures or in some ways makes less likely or less effective another activity" (Deutsch, 1973). Conflicts also have different levels of engagement in terms of what gets paid attention to and what is resolved. In a problem-solving approach to conflict, the presenting issue is what gets addressed. The conflict can be addressed by the people involved directly, or a third party intervener, such as a mediator, may be called in to assist (Lewicki, Saunders, & Minton, 2000/ 1997). In this case, single-loop learning is applied, as the way to amend the situation is by changing the behaviors or tactics being employed (Schon & Argyris, 1974; Marsick, 2000). A different approach, which is aimed at a deeper level of resolution, is the transformational; in this approach the relationship issues themselves, rather than the presenting issue, are addressed. In this situation, deciding what to address can best be determined by asking the following question: "What is this conflict REALLY about?" Here we see a transition from single- to double-loop learning in which the conceptual frameworks used to make the choices that apply in this situation are called into question. Basic assumptions are revealed and more attention is given to the underlying values and beliefs that govern those involved. Double-loop learning, which adds the component of critical reflection, brings into question the frames of reference we use to determine how we see, interpret, and make sense of the world around us (Arygyris & Schon, 1974; Mezirow, 1990; Marsick, 2000).

Research has shown that everyone who attends a conflict resolution workshop experiences some level of shift in their perspective from a new awareness, to a change in attitude, to changes that are actually manifested in behavioral differences (Fisher-Yoshida, 2000). These role plays and shared insights create opportunities for disorienting dilemmas to occur, what Mezirow (1990) claims to be the cornerstone of transformative learning. Brookfield (1987) believes that four steps are involved: identifying assumptions, checking their accuracy and validity, making alternative interpretations, and taking informed actions. He goes on to say that, "When we think critically, we come to judgments, choices and decisions for ourselves, instead of letting others do this on our behalf." Buber addresses the fact that there is a tension in which we may find ourselves as we try to hold on to our beliefs and still entertain the beliefs of the person with whom we are interacting (Fisher-Yoshida, 2003).

In organizations, communities, academic institutions, families, and other domains in which people gather together for specific purposes, there are many dynamics that contribute to the occurrence of conflict (Lewicki, Saunders, & Minton, 2000, 1997). These include inhibitors that prevent most people from proactively seeking ways to develop better interpersonal relationships. One of these inhibitors is the perceived power dynamics that take place between and among people at different levels within the organizational hierarchy. Conceptions of how you should behave in relation to your boss, colleague, direct report, or client impact the risk you are willing to take, with some of these attitudes and beliefs culturally influenced (Harris & Moran, 1979, 1987, 1991; Hofstede, 1991).

## Methodology for Conflict Management

Participants engaged in paired dialogues telling stories about conflicts they have had or are currently having and possible transformative moments they had about these conflicts. When their listening partner commented and openly questioned them about aspects of their conflict stories, the storytelling partner gained new insights and perspectives from which to view the conflict they had been living with for so long. This process was potentially transformative experience, as they considered their experiences in new ways. They often learned something about themselves or the other person that was an "eye opener" for them. This new learning was implemented with the introduction of theory and research to offer explanations as to why this happens (Mezirow, 1990; Bentz & Shapiro, 1998).

A second approach focused on learning and practicing skills that enable the participants to better manage future conflicts and their interpersonal interactions. This was effective as it honored the skill sets the participants brought with them by confirming what was already working well and by allowing them to acquire new skills to enhance the tools they already had. One of the purposes of introducing these particular skills is that we believed and research supports the fact that these skills when used are more likely to foster transformative learning experiences (Mezirow & Associates, 2000).

Communication is a critical factor in both helping to create and escalate conflicts and in working to resolve them. Dialogue is one type of communication that works very well in getting people to really "hear each other" and communicate to resolve their issues. "Dialogue is a dimension of communication quality that keeps communicators more focused on mutuality and relationship than on self-interest, more concerned with discovering than disclosing, more interested in access than in domination" (Anderson, Cissna, & Arnett, 1994). According to Isaacs (1999) there are four steps to fostering dialogue: an invitation to participate, generative listening in paying close attention to what is said, observing the observer in paying close attention to our own thoughts, and suspending our assumptions so we clearly listen to the whole story. People like to talk about themselves when there is an empathic listener on the receiving end. Thus the role of storytelling also became an important part of the paired experience the participants had in the workshop (Bentz & Shapiro, 1998). Dialogue is a tool or process that allows the participants to explore their differences and, at the same time, their common ground (Ellinor & Gerard, 1998). This provides the impetus for people in conflict to move closer together and realize they are not adversaries. "Dialogue calls attention to what communicators are making together" (Domenici & Littlejohn, 2000). Some term this "transformative dialogue" (Gergen, McNamee, & Barrett, 2001) in that it is an interchange that transforms a relationship into one in which common and solidifying realities are under construction.

## SUCCESSES IN SCHOLARLY PRACTITIONER APPLICATIONS: DEVELOPING RELATIONAL LEADERS

This application sought to provide a new perspective to the understanding of what is necessary to develop more capable, competent, and caring leaders for multinational corporations in the twenty-first century. As chief curriculum architect for one British multinational corporation's leadership development efforts my charter was to create a curriculum that would prepare leaders across the world (Asia, Africa, the Middle East, Europe, and the Americas) for the exigencies of the twenty-first century and to develop leaders to respond with agility and integrated responses to rapidly changing economic, social, and political situations. With greater recognition of complexity, ethical leaders are increasingly important in creating environments and cultures in which people recognize that a single right answer no longer exists, in which people feel valued for who they are and the talents they bring to the organization, in which others are freely and fully engaged in a common and higher purpose, and in which creativity flourishes and the spirit is free. Organizational survival depends on ethical managers and leaders who don't simply to ask *How do we do this?* and *Are we doing it right?* Managers and leaders in organizations that will survive need to let go of defensive routines and ask *Why are we doing this?* and *Are we doing the right things?* (Fulmer & Keys, 1998).

Leadership research shows that a sense of self and an authentic connection to others form the cornerstone for leadership in the twenty-first century (Burns, 1978; Bennis & Nanus, 1985; Kouzes & Posner 1987; Bass, Avolio, & Berson, 2003). And activities of care—being there, listening, the willingness to help, and the ability to understand—provide the basis for empowering both the self and the other (Gilligan, 1982; Noddings, 1984; Jordan et al., 1991). If the ethic of care can be learned, then organizations have the opportunity to develop a cadre of men and women with an increased capacity to build engagement through caring relationships with associates.

Finally, as organizations become truly global, "the other" must be considered as someone who is likely to be different from the self in gender, race, culture, geography and first language. In this setting the leader must learn how to value and validate the *other,* that is anyone who is different from the *self.* A leadership development program must acknowledge the impact of culture and raise awareness of how the context and confluence of diversity serve a necessary and transformational role for those who are leaders in global corporations.

Brown and Posner (2001, p. 279) explored the relationship between transformative learning and transformational leadership and concluded that leadership development programs and approaches need to reach leaders at a personal and emotional level, triggering critical self-reflection, providing support for meaning making, creating learning and leadership mindsets, and allowing time for experimentation. They propose that transformative learning theory be used to assess, strengthen, and create leadership development programs that develop transformational leaders.

## Methodology for Successful Relational Leadership Programs

Through the development of relational leadership capabilities an organization establishes a common foundation for increasing levels of reflective action, intercultural appreciation, employee engagement, and ethical action, all of which may positively influence business performance. Relational leadership development programs tailored to incorporate and support a multinational corporation's values, strategic intent, business goals, and performance management approach are designed to build leaders who are able to question assumptions, accept diverse perspectives; broaden the understanding of situations, consider the complex interrelationships that impact business decisions, and gain more self-understanding (Geller, 2004). A few examples of transformative learning interventions will be provided. None of these experiences alone is enough; each involves larger learning interventions that are intentionally designed to develop the ability to tailor relational leadership practices to specific contexts.

*Experiencing a Multifaceted Self*

Leadership development programs traditionally incorporate use of a psychological survey (e.g., MBTI, Motivation Orientation, Social Styles, ACUMEN), measures of leadership (e.g., MLQ, LPI, Situational Leadership Survey), or to some extent 360° feedback (e.g., Benchmarks, Profilor or tailored questionnaires). Leaders from a number of prominent organizations have stated that when they consider prior leadership programs they realize that the results from these surveys have provided lasting information; for some this represents the most meaningful contribution of these efforts.

Relational leadership development suggests the need to understand the self and other by incorporating multiple ways of building self-awareness and recognizing similarities and differences. Fostering relational leadership development through surveys, questionnaires, and 360° feedback continues to hold value by providing insight into the self and the other. The differentiating factor in a relational leadership development intervention is the acknowledgment and appreciation of the complexity of people. To honor this complexity, one survey view is not enough. Understanding the self and other is better done by combining and offering a broad range of tools and experiences each showing a "snapshot" of the individual. In synthesizing these "snapshots" a more comprehensive and "three-dimensional" view of the leader emerges. The acquisition of these insights in a communal setting fostering reflection and dialogue leads to an awareness and appreciation of the full range of values, beliefs, attitudes, and behavior for the self and for acceptance of others.

*Creating Learning Partnerships That Frame*
*the Experience of Mindful Interactions*

Creating learning partnerships in the context of a relational leadership development intervention is a way of showing the importance of developing meaningful interactions with the other. Through the design of a structured interview leaders gain an appreciative view of the other. The interview identifies what the leader is currently doing that supports these practices and indirectly provides information on opportunities in which the individual can increase their use. The learning partnership provides each person with a view of themselves through the eyes of the other—an interested but dispassionate person who sees both positive and negative in a broader context. The partnership is a supportive affiliation for learning in which encouragement and challenge are given and received in confidence. As the partner is generally a colleague in the same organization, there is shared knowledge of the contextual realities of the work setting.

The initial process with those in partnership is as important as the interviews themselves; it is about establishing a mutually responsive and empathic relationship. Partners are asked to hold conversations to share insights about themselves, are encouraged to set ground rules for how they will work together, and commit to a plan of action that each agrees to fulfil for the other. Setting a context is a critical part of the preinterview process and the partners are encouraged to share background information on their leadership performance.

The partner personally contacts the people identified by the other and conducts conversations to gain answers to the agreed upon questions. The interviewer must then consider and synthesize these data in preparation for sharing the data in a one-on-one extended conversation held within a larger learning intervention. The two share their insights and gain increased awareness of how each as a person and a leader is experienced by others. The conversations require mindfulness of the other, empathy and mutual responsiveness, respect and even appreciation for difference, an ethical approach to confidentiality, and naturally incorporate elements of dialogue.

*Using Art as a Means to Learn about the Self,*
*Other, and Practices of Relationship*

Art is a powerful and creative way to take a group to a deeper understanding of the interplay of the self and the other. Because masks play an important role in so many cultures, a mask-making activity is generally accepted by participants from a range of cultures, although it is a challenge as it is generally outside the current comfort zones of most people. Because it is a very personal and even intimate activity people must be willing to "trust the process" and honor each other. Incorporating this experience assumes that a foundation for trust and care has previously been established.

Using plaster cast materials and working with partners, each person creates a form of the other's face. This is a highly personal process and it is necessary to be mindful of the other's thoughts— "can I allow myself to be touched," "am I claustrophobic," "will I be able to breath"—and the self's thoughts as well—"is this mask good enough," "am I doing it right," "I've never touched another man's face before." The activity requires empathic responsiveness to the other. Because it is a two-way process in which each partner makes a mask on (and for) the other, mutuality and care are essential.

After decorating a leader describes several elements of his or her own mask and suggests what those elements represent ("I put yellow paint on first because I wanted the mask to be sunny, but it didn't look right, so then I layered on other colors and as I think about it, it's like there is this sunshine hidden behind other things"). Others in the group are invited to say what they see in a mask, but not to make judgments about it: "I'm struck by your use of only black and white." "Your mask seems to have two sides." "Your mask is mysterious." The process creates a safe context in which people can explore their own personalities with others through art.

Throughout the experience, people have simply "trusted the process." At its conclusion leaders note the value of developing an evolving sense of self experienced within the context of the other. They have developed an appreciation of the thinking and feeling behind the faces of others and have built a sense of communal "we-ness."

## CONCLUSIONS

We found that leading participants through the experience of one-to-one dialogues, storytelling, skill building, and constructive feedback enables them to experience their situations in different and sometimes transformative ways. Participants no longer view themselves in the same way they did when they first entered the workshops. This transformation may also enable them to view the other people with whom they interact in new ways. It also provides a framework from which they can view future situations, enabling them to embrace perspectives different from the ones they usually hold.

The opportunity to sit back and experience guided reflection allows the participants to gain new insights about themselves. Schon (1983) talks about theories in action (what is actually being used) as compared to espoused theories (those that we say we apply, but don't). When people have the chance to reflect on action, they will be better prepared to act in action, resulting in a better alignment between the theories in action and those espoused.

Do these workshops resolve all conflicts, change all perspectives, or develop truly relational leadership? No. Do the participants leave so highly skilled that they will manage every subsequent relationship better than before? Not necessarily. What these interventions do is equip the participants with new tools that enable them to vary their techniques. It allows the participants to take increasing ownership of their situations and the choices they make, with the full knowledge that there are consequences to every choice. Based on our experience and the testimonials of participants, this process is both exciting and empowering.

# ENDNOTES

## CHAPTER 1

1. Indian political and spiritual leader (1869–1948).
2. Palmisano, S. J. (2006). Multinationals have been superseded. *Financial Times*, London (UK), June 12, p. 19. Palmisano, S. J. (2006). The globally integrated enterprise. *Foreign Affairs*, *85(3)*, 127.
3. Drucker, P. F. (1987). Drucker on management: The transnational economy. *Wall Street Journal*, August 25, p. 1.
4. Palmisano, S. J. (2006). The globally integrated enterprise. *Foreign Affairs*, *85(3)*, 127.
5. *Stanford Encyclopedia of Philosophy*, June 2006.
6. *Stanford Encyclopedia of Philosophy*, June 2006.
7. Globalization Website, Department of Sociology, Emory University.
8. http://www.yourpointofview.com/ February 10, 2008.
9. American Society for Training and Development (ASTD), *State of the Industry 2006 Report*.
10. Center for Creative Leadership. (2003). *Handbook of leadership development*. San Francisco, CA: Jossey-Bass.
11. "Where will we find tomorrow's leaders?" A conversation with Linda A. Hill. *Harvard Business Review, Special HBS Centennial Issue*, January 2008.
12. Adler, N. (2008). *International dimensions of organizational behavior*, 5th ed. Mason, OH: Thompson South-Western.
13. Geller, K. D. (2004). *A model of relational leadership development for multinational corporations in the 21st century*. Ph.D. Thesis, Fielding Graduate University. Bass, B. M. & Avolio, B. J. (1994). *Improving organizational effectiveness through transformational leadership*. Thousand Oaks, CA: Sage Publications.
14. Landis, D., Bennett, J.M., & Bennett, M.J. (2004). *Handbook of intercultural training*. Thousand Oaks, CA: Sage Publications.
15. Our back office operations are outsourced to certain locations in the world that may not be where we are physically located; our call centers have also been outsourced, so that a person calling for technical support in Chicago in the United States could very well dial a toll free number and be speaking to someone in Chennai, India.

16. Mezirow, J. (2000). Learning to think like an adult: Core concepts of transformation theory. In J. Mezirow (Ed.), *Learning as transformation: Critical perspectives on a theory in progress.* San Francisco, CA: Jossey-Bass.

17. Bennett, M.J. (1998). Intercultural communication: A current perspective. In M. J. Bennett (Ed.), *Basic concepts of intercultural communication.* Yarmouth, ME: Intercultural Press.

# CHAPTER 2

1. Traditional text said to have been written by the Taoist, Lao Tzu, which means "old master." It dates to the sixth century BC.

2. Boyatzis, R. E., & McKee, A. (2005). *Resonant leadership: Renewing yourself and connecting with others through mindfulness, hope, and compassion.* Boston, MA: Harvard Business School Press.

3. Hall, E. T. (1992). *Beyond culture.* Gloucester, MA: Peter Smith Publishers.

4. Hofstede, G. (2004). *Cultures and organizations: Software of the mind.* New York: McGraw-Hill.

5. Hampden-Turner, C., & Trompenaars, F. (1997). *Riding the waves of culture: Understanding diversity in global business,* 2nd ed. New York: McGraw-Hill.

6. This is based on extensive survey work conducted by Henry Cantril in the 1950s and 1960s drawing on populations in Italy, France, Russia, Poland, India, Egypt, Nigeria, Brazil, the Dominican Republic, and others.

7. Hampden-Turner, C., & Trompenaars, F. (1997). *Riding the waves of culture: Understanding diversity in global business,* 2nd ed. New York: McGraw-Hill.

8. Kouzes, J. M., & Posner, B. Z. (2007). *The leadership challenge,* 4th ed. San Francisco, CA: Jossey-Bass.

9. Tajfel, H. (1974). Social identity and intergroup behaviour. *Social Science Information, 13,* 65–93.

10. Tajfel, H., & Turner, J. C. (1986). The social identity theory of inter-group behavior. In S. Worchel & L. W. Austin (Eds.), *Psychology of intergroup relations.* Chigago: Nelson-Hall.

11. Huddy, L. (2001). From social to political identity: A critical examination of social identity theory. *Political Psychology, 22(1),* 127–156. DOI: 10.1111/0162-895X.00230.

12. Garcia-Prieto, P., Bellard, E., & Schneider, S. (2003). Experiencing diversity, conflict, and emotions in teams. *Applied Psychology, 52(3),* 413-440. DOI: 10.1111/1464-0597.00142.

13. Pizarro, M., & Vera, E. M. (2001). Chicano/a ethnic identity research. *The Counseling Psychologist, 29(1),* 91–117. DOI: 10.1177/0011000001291004.

14. Kumar, R., & Nti, K. O. (2004). National cultural values and the evolution of process and outcome discrepancies in international strategic alliances. *The Journal of Applied Behavioral Science, 40(3),* 344–361.

15. Murata, K. (2007). Unanswered questions: Cultural assumptions in text interpretation. *International Journal of Applied Linguistics, 17(1),* 38–59. DOI: 10.1111/j.1473-4192.2007.00132.x.

16. Bennett, M. J. (1986). A developmental approach to training for intercultural sensitivity. *International Journal of Intercultural Relations, 10(2),* 179–195; Merriam, S. B., Caffarella, R. S., & Baumgarten, L. M. (2006). *Learning in adulthood: A comprehensive guide.* San Francisco, CA: Jossey-Bass.

17. Mezirow, J. (2000). *Learning as transformation: Critical perspectives on a theory in progress.* San Francisco, CA: Jossey-Bass.

18. Senge, P., Kleiner, A., Roberts, C., Roth, G., Ross, R., & Smith, B. (1999). *The dance of change: The challenges to sustaining momentum in learning organizations.* New York: Doubleday.

# CHAPTER 3

1. Hofstede, G. (2004). *Cultures and organizations: Software of the mind.* New York: McGraw-Hill.

2. Harper, A. (2007). *Doing business across cultures.* Unpublished paper. Hall, E. T., & Hall, M. R. (1990). *Understanding cultural differences.* Yarmouth, ME: Intercultural Press.

3. Ho, D. Y.-F. (1976). On the concept of face. *American Journal of Sociology, 81(4),* 867–884.

4. *http://www.expat.or.id/business/facetoshame.html.*

5. Kolb, D. A., & Osland, J. (2006). *Organizational behavior: An experiential approach.* Harlow: Prentice Hall.

6. Daniels, A. C. (2004). *Performance management: Changing behavior that drives organizational effectiveness.* Atlanta, GA: Performance Management Publications.

# CHAPTER 4

1. Peter Drucker (1909–2005) was a well-known writer, management consultant and university professor.

2. Link, P. (1992). Evening chats in Beijing: Probing China's predicament, p. 64. New York: Norton.

3. Boyatzis, R. E., & McKee, A. (2005). *Resonant leadership: Renewing yourself and connecting with others through mindfulness, hope, and compassion.* Cambridge, MA: Harvard Business School Press.

4. Hall, E. T. (1966). *The hidden dimension.* New York: Doubleday.

5. Hofstede, G. (1991). *Software of the mind.* New York: McGraw-Hill.

6. Murray, D. P. (1983). Face to face: American and Chinese interactions. In R. A. Kapp (Ed.), *Communicating with change,* pp. 9–27. Yarmouth, ME: Intercultural Press.

7. Saying words such as "perhaps" is understood as being a face-saving "no." The Chinese understand this, but it may pass right over the heads of the Americans. There are other face-saving ways in which dissent is communicated; in Japan, for example, support is gathered before the meeting so there is no face-harming potential resulting from someone springing a surprise at the meeting.

8. Ferguson, S. D. (1988). Organizational theory and its communication implications. In S. D. Ferguson & S. Ferguson (Eds.), *Organizational communication,* 2nd ed. Edison, NJ: Transaction Publishers.

# CHAPTER 5

1. Marsick, V. J. (1990). Action learning and reflection in the workplace. In J. Mezirow (Ed.), *Fostering critical reflection in adulthood: A guide for transformative and emancipatory learning*, p. 23. San Francisco, CA: Jossey-Bass.

2. Argyris, C. (1993). *Knowledge in action: A guide to overcoming barriers to organizational change*. San Francisco, CA: Jossey-Bass. Fulmer, R., & Keyes, J. (1998). A conversation with Chris Argyris: The father of organizational learning. *Organizational Dynamics, 27(2)*, 21–32.

3. We discussed having voice in Chapter 4, Paradox of Communication.

4. We discussed this more thoroughly in Chapter 4, Paradox of Communication.

5. Hofstede, G. (1984). *Culture's consequences: International differences in work-related values*. Newbury Park, CA: Sage Publications.

6. Hampden-Turner, C., & Trompenaars, F. (2000). *Building cross-cultural competence: How to create wealth from conflicting values*. New Haven, CT: Yale University Press.

# CHAPTER 6

1. Böhm, S., Herrmann, C., & Trinczek, R. (2004). *Herausforderung Vertrauensarbeitszeit zur Kultur und Praxis eines neuen Arbeitszeitmodells*. Berlin, Sigma.

2. Hampden-Turner, C., & Trompenaars, F. (2000). *Building cross-cultural competence: How to create wealth from conflicting values*. New Haven, CT: Yale University Press.

3. Hampden-Turner, C., & Trompenaars, F. (2000). *Building cross-cultural competence: How to create wealth from conflicting values*. New Haven, CT: Yale University Press.

4. Hall, E. T. (1996). *Dance of life*. Gloucester, MA: Peter Smith Publishers.

5. Hampden-Turner, C., & Trompenaars, F. (2000). *Building cross-cultural competence: How to create wealth from conflicting values*. New Haven, CT: Yale University Press.

6. Senge, P., Scharmer, C. O., Jaworski, J., & Flowers, B. S. (2005). *Presence*. Boston, MA: Nicholas Brealey Publishers.

7. Corporate Environmental Responsibility: Is a common CSR framework possible? P. Mazurkiewicz, Development Committee, World Bank, 2004.

8. World Bank, 2004.

9. Boston College, Carroll School of Management, Center for Corporate Citizenship, 2008.

10. www.earthwatch.org.

11. This is why it is important to refer back to estimating the long-term impact of decisions that do not only focus on the short term. There is growing concern **among different** groups around the world about the environment and the threat of global warming. This movement is growing and many people are no longer comfortable putting off difficult decisions that will affect their children and grandchildren. Instead they are calling for accountability from corporations. Citizens are holding businesses responsible and are taking grass root actions to enforce their beliefs and as a call to action. *www.earthwatch.org.*

# CHAPTER 7

1. *"Child's Pose"* or *"Balasana"* is a yoga pose that allows for rest and rejuvenation. It is done between other more strenuous yoga poses to allow for a cycle of strengthening, increasing flexibility, and mindful relaxation and mediation. It supports energy flow throughout the mind and body. www.yogajournal.com.

2. Gladwell, M. (2002). *The tipping point: How little things can make a big difference.* New York: Back Bay Books, Hachette Publishing.

3. Brookfield, S. (1991). *Understanding and facilitating adult learning: A comprehensive analysis of principles and effective practices.* San Francisco, CA: Jossey-Bass. Merriam, S., Caffarella, R., & Baumgartner, L. (2006). *Learning in adulthood: A comprehensive guide.* San Francisco, CA: Jossey-Bass.

4. Kolb, D. Learning style inventory.

5. In Appendix 2 there is information on the online survey available for assessing your current status of addressing the five paradoxes of transnational leadership. Please follow the directions for completing this form online to receive your results. You are also helping to support our data collection, which will support the validation of the survey instrument.

# APPENDIX 2

1. Brooks, A. K. (2004). Transformational learning theory and implications for human resource development. *Advances in Developing Human Resources, 6(2),* 211–225.

# REFERENCES

Adler, N. J. (1991). *International dimensions of organizational behavior.* The Kent international dimensions of business series. Boston, MA: PWS-KENT Pub.

Anderson, R., & Cissna, K. N. (2002). *Moments of meeting: Buber, Rogers and the potential for public dialogue.* Albany, NY: State University of New York Press.

Argyris, C. (1993). *Knowledge in action: A guide to overcoming barriers to organizational change.* San Francisco, CA: Jossey-Bass.

Argyris, C., & Schon, D. (1974). *Theory in practice: Increasing professional effectiveness.* San Francisco, CA: Jossey-Bass.

Arnett, R.C., & Arneson, P. (1999). *Dialogic civility in a cynical age: Community, hope and interpersonal relationships.* Albany, NY: State University of New York Press.

Barnlund, D. C. (1989). *Public and private self in Japan and the United States: Communicative styles of two cultures.* Yarmouth, ME: Intercultural Press.

Bass, B. M., & Avolio, B. J. (Eds.). (1994). *Improving organizational effectiveness through transformational leadership.* Thousand Oaks, CA: Sage Publications.

Bass, B. M., Avolio, B. J., Jung, D. I., & Berson, Y. (2003). Predicting unit performance by assessing transformational and transactional leadership. *Journal of Applied Psychology, 88(2 April),* 207–218.

Bennett, M. J. (1986). A developmental approach to training for intercultural sensitivity. *International Journal of Intercultural Relations, 10(2),* 179–195.

Bennett, M. J. (ed.) (1998). *Basic concepts of intercultural communication.* Yarmouth, ME: Intercultural Press.

Bennis, W., & Nanus, B. (1985). *Leaders: The strategies for taking charge.* New York: Harper & Row.

Bentz, V. M.. & Shapiro, J. (1998). *Mindful inquiry in social research.* Thousand Oaks, CA: Sage Publications.

Bohm, D. (1996). In L. Nichols (Ed.), *On dialogue.* London: Routledge Press.

Böhm, S., Herrmann, C., & Trinczek, R. (2004). *Herausforderung Vertrauensarbeitszeit zur Kultur und Praxis eines neuen Arbeitszeitmodells.* Berlin, Sigma.

Bond, M. (1991). *Beyond the Chinese face.* Hong Kong: Oxford University Press.

Boston College, Carroll School of Management, Center for Corporate Citizenship, 2008.

Boyatzis, R. E., & McKee, A. (2005). *Resonant leadership: Renewing yourself and connecting with others through mindfulness, hope, and compassion.* Boston: Harvard Business School Press.

Brookfield, S. D. (1987). *Developing critical thinkers: Challenging adults to explore alternative ways of thinking and acting.* San Francisco, CA: Jossey-Bass.

Brookfield, S. (1991). *Understanding and facilitating adult learning: A comprehensive analysis of principles and effective practices.* San Francisco, CA: Jossey-Bass.

Brooks, A. K. (2004). Transformational learning theory and implications for human resource development. *Advances in Developing Human Resources, 6(2),* 211–225.

Brown, L. M., & Posner, B. Z. (2001). Exploring the relationship between learning and leadership. *Leadership and Organization Development Journal, 22(5),* 274–280.

Buber, M. (1996). *I and thou.* Walter Kaufmann (Trans.) New York: Simon & Schuster.

Burns, J. M. (1978). *Leadership.* New York: Harper & Row.

Caffarella, R., & Baumgartner, L. (2006*). Learning in adulthood: A comprehensive guide.* San Francisco, CA: Jossey-Bass.

Cantril, H. (1965). *The pattern of human concerns.* New Brunswick, NJ: Rutgers University Press.

Chavez, A.F., Guido-DeBrito, F., & Mallory, S. (2006). Learning to value the other: A model of diversity development. Unpublished paper cited in Merriam, S. B., & Caffarella, R. S. *Learning in adulthood a comprehensive guide.* The Jossey-Bass higher and adult education series. San Francisco, CA: Jossey-Bass.

Coleman, P. (2003). An outsider's reflections on the relationship between transformative learning and conflict. *Transformative Learning Conference,* Teachers College, Columbia University, New York.

Cooperrider, D., & Srivastva, S. (2001). Appreciative inquiry in organizational life. In D. Cooperrider, P. Sorensen, Jr., T. Yaeger, & D. Whitney (Eds.), *Appreciative inquiry: An emerging direction for organization development.* Champaign, IL: Stipes Publishing.

Covey, S. R. (2004). *The 8ᵗʰ habit: From effectiveness to greatness.* New York: Free Press.

Daniels, A. C. (2004). *Performance management: Changing behavior that drives organizational effectiveness.* Atlanta, GA: Performance Management Publications.

Deutsch, M. (1973). *The resolution of conflict: Constructive and destructive processes.* New Haven, CT: Yale University Press.

Dirx, J. M. (1997). Nurturing soul in adult learning. In P. Cranton (Ed.), *Transformative learning in action: Insights from practice.* San Francisco, CA: Jossey-Bass.

Drucker, P. F. (1971). *Drucker on management.* [London]: Management Publications Limited.

Ellinor, L., & Gerard, G. (1998). *Dialogue: Rediscovering the transforming power of conversation.* New York: John Wiley & Sons, Inc.

Emory University, Globalization Website, p. 3. Accessed March 2, 2008. http://www.sociology.emory.edu/globalization/data.html#culture.

Fisher-Yoshida, B. (2000). Altering awareness of self, relationship and context in conflict resolution: Impact, feedback and reflection. *Dissertation Abstracts International, 61/03,* 1694B (UMI No. 9966201).

Fisher-Yoshida, B. (2003). Self-awareness and the co-construction of conflict. *Human Systems: The Journal of Systemic Consultation & Management, 14(2),* 3–22.

Freire, P. (1970). *Pedagogy of the oppressed.* New York: Herter and Herter.

Gao, G., & Ting-Toomey, S. (1998). *Communicating effectively with the Chinese.* Thousand Oaks, CA: Sage Publications.

Garcia-Prieto, P., Bellard, E., & Schneider, S. (2003). Experiencing diversity, conflict, and emotions in teams. *Applied Psychology, 52(3),* 413–440. DOI: 10.1111/1464-0597.00142.

Geller, K. D. (2004). *A model of relational leadership development for multinational corporations in the 21st century.* Ph.D. Thesis, Fielding Graduate Institute.

Gilligan, C. (1982). *In a different voice: Psychological theory and women's development.* Cambridge, MA: Harvard University Press.

Gladwell, M. (2002). *The tipping point: How little things can make a big difference.* New York: Back Bay Books, Hachette Publishing.

Gudykunst, W. B., Ting-Toomey, S., & Nishida, T. (Eds.). (1996). *Communication in personal relationships across cultures.* Thousand Oaks, CA: Sage Publications.

Hall E. T. (1959). *The silent language.* New York: Doubleday.

Hall, E. T. (1992). *Beyond culture.* Gloucester, MA: Peter Smith Publishers.

Hall, E. T. (1996). *Dance of life.* Gloucester, MA: Peter Smith Publishers.

Hall, E. T., & Hall, M. R. (1990). *Understanding cultural differences.* Yarmouth, ME: Intercultural Press.

Hampden-Turner, C., & Trompenaars, F. (1997). *Riding the waves of culture: Understanding diversity in global business,* 2nd ed. New York: McGraw-Hill.

Hampden-Turner, C., & Trompenaars, F. (2000). *Building cross-cultural competence: How to create wealth from conflicting values.* New Haven, CT: Yale University Press.

Hannum, K. M. (2007). *Social identity: knowing yourself, leading others.* Greensboro, NC: Center for Creative Leadership.

Harper, A. (2007). *Doing business across cultures.* Unpublished paper. Cultural Shapeshifters Pty. Ltd.

Harris, P. T., & Moran, R. T. (1979, 1987, 1991). *Managing cultural differences: High performance strategies for a new world of business.* Houston, TX: Gulf Publishing.

Ho, D. Y. (1976). "On the Concept of Face." *American Journal of Sociology, 81(4),* 867–884.

Hofstede, G. (1984). *Culture's consequences: International differences in work-related values.* Newbury Park, CA: Sage, Publications.

Hofstede, G. (2004). *Cultures and organizations: Software of the mind.* New York: McGraw-Hill.

HSBC. (2008). Your point of view website. Accessed March 2 , 2008, http://www.yourpoint ofview.com/.

Huddy, L. (2001). From social to political identity: A critical examination of social identity Theory. *Political Psychology, 22(1),* 127–156. DOI: 10.1111/0162-895X.00230.

Isaacs, W. (1999). *Dialogue and the art of thinking together: A pioneering approach to communicating in business and in life.* New York: Currency.

Jordan, J., Kaplan, A., Miller, J. B., Stiver, I., & Surrey, J. (1991). *Women's growth in connection: Writings from the Stone Center.* New York: The Guildford Press.

Kasl, E., & Yorks, L. (2002). An epistemology for transformative learning theory and its application through collaborative inquiry. *TCRecord.org.* Retrieved 1/28/02: http://222.tcrecord .org.content ID10877.

Kegan, R. (1982). *The evolving self: Problem and process in human development.* Cambridge, MA: Harvard University Press.

Kegan, R., & Leahy, L. L. (2001). *How the way we talk can change the way we work: Seven languages for transformation.* San Francisco, CA: Jossey-Bass.

Kolb, D. A. (1976). *The Learning Style Inventory: Technical manual,* Boston, MA: McBer.

Kolb, D. A., & Osland, J. (2006). *Organizational behavior: An experiential approach.* Harlow: Prentice-Hall.

Kouzes, J. M., & Posner, B. Z. (2007). *The leadership challenge,* 4th ed. San Francisco, CA: Jossey-Bass.

Kumar, R., & Nti, K. O. (2004). National cultural values and the evolution of process and outcome discrepancies in international strategic alliances. *The Journal of Applied Behavioral Science, 40(3)*, 344–361.

Laozi, F., & English, J. (1972). *Tao te ching*. New York: Vintage Books.

Lewicki, R. J., Saunders, D. M., & Minton, J. W. (2000, 1997). *Essentials of negotiation*, 2nd ed. Boston: McGraw-Hill Irwin.

Link, P. (1992). *Evening chats in Beijing: Probing China's predicament*. New York: Norton.

Littlejohn, S. W., & Domenici, K. (2001). *Engaging communication in conflict: Systemic practice*. Thousand Oaks, CA: Sage Publications.

Marsick, V. J. (1990). Action learning and reflection in the workplace. In J. Mezirow (Ed.), *Fostering critical reflection in adulthood: A guide for transformative and emancipatory learning*. San Francisco, CA: Jossey-Bass.

Marsick, V. J., & Cederhom, L. (1989). Developing leadership in international managers—an urgent challenge. *Columbia Journal of World Business, 23(4)*, 3–11.

Marsick, V. J., & Sauquet, A. (2000). Learning through reflection. In *The handbook of conflict resolution: Theory and practice*. San Francisco, CA: Jossey-Bass.

Mazurkiewicz, P. (2004). *Corporate environmental responsibility*. Development Committee, World Bank.

McCauley, C. D., Moxley, R. S., & Van Velsor, E. (1998). *The Center for Creative Leadership handbook of leadership development*. San Francisco, CA: Jossey-Bass.

Merriam, S. B., Caffarella, R. S., & Baumgartner, L. (2006). *Learning in adulthood: A comprehensive guide*, 3rd ed. San Francisco, CA: Jossey - Bass.

Mezirow, J. (1990). In J. Mezirow (Ed.), *Fostering critical reflection in adulthood: A guide to emancipatory learning*. San Francisco, CA: Jossey-Bass.

Mezirow, J. (1991). *Transformative dimensions of adult learning*. San Francisco, CA: Jossey-Bass.

Mezirow, J. (2000). In J. Mezirow (Ed.), *Learning as transformation: Critical perspectives on a theory in progress*. San Francisco, CA: Jossey-Bass.

Murata, K. (2007). Unanswered questions: Cultural assumptions in text interpretation *International Journal of Applied Linguistics, 17(1)*, 38–59. DOI: 10.1111/j.1473-4192.2007.00132.x.

Murray, D. P. (1983). Face to face: American and Chinese interactions. In Robert A. Kapp (Ed.), *Communicating with change*, pp. 9–27 . Chicago, IL: Intercultural Press.

Noddings, N. (2003). *Caring: A feminist approach to ethics and moral education*, 2nd edition. Berkeley, CA: University of California Press.

Palmisano, S. J. (2006). Multinationals have been superseded, *Financial Times*, (UK) June 12, p. 19

Palmisano, S. J. (2006). The globally integrated enterprise. *Foreign Affairs, 85(3)*, 127.

Pearce, W. B., & Pearce, K. A. (2000). Combining passions and abilities toward dialogic virtuosity. *Southern Communication Journal, 65*, 161–175.

Pfeffer, J. (1994). *Competitive advantage through people*. Boston: Harvard Business School Press.

Pizarro, M., & Vera, E. M. (2001). Chicana/o ethnic identify research: lessons for researchers and counselors. *The Counseling Psychologist, 29(1)*, 91–117. DOI: 10.1177/0011000001291004.

Schein, E. H. (1988). *Process consultation: Its role in organization development*. Reading, MA: Addison-Wesley Publishing Company.

Schein, E. H. (2004). *Organizational culture and leadership*, 3rd ed. San Francisco, CA: Jossey-Bass.

Schon, D. (1983). *The reflective practitioner: How professionals think in action*. New York: Basic Books.

Schön, D. A. (1995). *Educating the reflective practitioner: Toward a new design for teaching and learning in the professions.* San Francisco, CA: Jossey-Bass.

Seashore, C. N., Seashore, E. W., & Weinberg, G. M. (1992, 1996,1997). *What did you say? The art of giving and receiving feedback.* Columbia, MD: Bingham House Books.

Senge, P. M. (1999). *The dance of change: The challenges of sustaining momentum in learning organizations.* New York: Currency/Doubleday.

Senge, P. M. (2006). *The fifth discipline: The art and practice of the learning organization.* London: Random House Business.

Senge, P., Scharmer, C. O., Jaworski, J., & Flowers, B. S. (2005). *Presence.* Boston, MA: Nicholas Brealey Publishers.

Stanford University & Center for the Study of Language and Information (U.S.). (1997). *Stanford encyclopedia of philosophy.* Stanford, CA: Stanford University. http://plato.stanford.edu/.

Tajfel, H. (1974). Social identity and intergroup behaviour. *Social Science Information, 13,* 65–93.

Tajfel, H., & Turner, J. C. (1986). The social identity theory of inter-group behavior. In S. Worchel & L. W. Austin (Eds.), *Psychology of Intergroup Relations.* Chicago, IL: Nelson-Hall.

Tannen, D. (1999). *The argument culture: Stopping America's war of words.* New York: Ballantine Books.

Taylor, E. W. (1994). Intercultural competency: A transformative learning process. *Adult Education Quarterly, 44(3),* 154–174.

Taylor, E. W. (2000). Analyzing research on transformative learning theory. In J. Mezirow (Ed.), *Learning as transformation: Critical perspectives on a theory in progress.* San Francisco, CA: Jossey-Bass.

Taylor, E. W. (2003). *Looking back five years: A critical review of transformative learning theory.* Paper presented at the Columbia Teachers College Conference on Transformative Learning. New York: Columbia University.

Trompenaars, F., & Hampden-Turner, C. (2004),. *Managing people across cultures.* West Sussex, England: Capstone.

The Quotations Page. (2008). http://www.quotationspage.com. Accessed March 2, 2008.

Wei-Ming, T. (1995). *The living tree: The changing meaning of being Chinese today.* Stanford, CA: Stanford University Press.

A link to the survey developed by the authors for *Transnational Leadership Development* can be found at: http://www.surveymonkey.com/s.aspx?sm=oVV9Pv72H2_2fb xXdPJJnLiQ_3d_3d

# ACKNOWLEDGMENTS

We began the preface by stating that the world was becoming a global village. Perhaps the reason we feel this way comes in part from our experience in working collaboratively while living and working on two sides of the world—10,000 miles and 12 time zones apart. From VOIP conversations to meetings in New York, Santa Barbara, Hong Kong, Dubai, Nairobi, Accra, Singapore, Johannesburg, and Helsinki, the creation of this book has been its own transnational journey.

In this world context, we have come to appreciate each other. Close to the conclusion of the book one of our colleagues, Audrey Charlton, asked Beth how our writing together was working. Knowing us both, Audrey knew that we had very different styles—thinking, speaking, facilitating and writing—and was surprised when Beth said that "it's really great." In this collaborative process, we have come to know ourselves and each other better. Rather than reacting to our differences, we learned to appreciate what each of us brought to the story that we tell here. We couldn't be more complementary partners in our work together.

Our journey began when we met in Santa Barbara, California, while attending sessions at Fielding Graduate University where we both obtained doctorates in Human and Organizational Systems. This is where we both first encountered transformative learning and relational leadership as fields of study. Our journey continued when we entertained becoming coauthors in October 2005 at the Sixth Biannual Transformative Learning Conference held at Michigan State. Between sessions, we found ourselves sharing ideas with Victoria Marsick, discovering in the conversation that Victoria was coeditor for this series. As the conversation neared its conclusion, Victoria offered to send us the "Manuscript Submission Guidelines." From then on she has worked with us, and from that first conversation, she has been a source of encouragement. From sharing her ideas on reflection in the workplace to reviewing our draft manuscript, we appreciate the role Victoria has played on our journey.

As our journey was ending, we thought about who could write a foreword for our book. Janet Bennett's name stood out from among many. Besides being a well-known interculturalist with whom we have personally learned and developed, we continuously evoked her spirit in our workshops by quoting her and her teachings. We thought we could evoke her spirit in a more prominent position by asking her to be a part of the writing, and she so graciously agreed to fit us into her hectic globetrotting schedule by writing the foreword. We are grateful and thank you Janet.

A book is only a series of typed pages until the editors join into the conversation. It was with the blessing of the Series Editors— Andrea Ellinger, Victoria Marsick, and William Rothwell—that we began this project. And it is under the guidance of Jacqueline Flynn (and her capable team) that we brought this project from paper to printed book! We appreciate the wisdom and knowledge that have been shared during the course of the project.

There are leaders, managers, colleagues, and friends too numerous to mention who told us stories of their challenges, shared their triumphs, and reflected on their errors. Our stories are composites of these voices, reflecting true experiences where sometimes we learned. Other times, the learning happened many months or even years after the conversation. To each leader who touched our lives, thank you for sharing your authentic selves, your lives, and your experiences.

We would be remiss if we failed to acknowledge our families and friends who stood by us through this process.

## A FEW NOTES OF APPRECIATION FROM BETH

The journey that brings me here today goes back to my earliest memories. I do remember being constantly curious, and this questioning and yearning has taken me to many corners of the world. Growing up in New York City provided the background for developing the traits of assertiveness and independence that have aided me in all my endeavors. I value the 13 years I lived, worked, and studied in Japan because it tempered my impatience and allowed me to learn to sit with silence. Sometimes.

I want to thank my parents, Frieda and Seymour Fisher, who always believed in me and knew I could do and be anything I wanted in the world; my best friend, my sister Mindy, who is always there to share laughs, tears, and oh so many adventures; and my fabulous daughters, Ria and Aya, who always make me proud of them. Their wit, charm, talent, and sense of adventure keep me on my toes. Thanks also to my niece Erin and nephew Justin, who are deep in my heart—our family vacations are incomparable; my wonderful husband and other best friend, Malick, who makes it easy for me to be me, with his constant love, support, and ways of keeping it lively to keep me going; and to all my family and friends, Susan, Adam, and Nicola Gebler, Marcia Levy, Charlie Bernstein, Adair Nagata, Helen Matsuki, Teri & Jeff Axel, Donna & Barry Sommers, Cathy Seidel, and everyone else who know they are dear to me, thank you.

I want to acknowledge my mentors and friends at Fielding Graduate University, Barnett Pearce, Libby Douvan, Jeremy Shapiro, Janja Lallich, Steve Schapiro, Martha Sherman, Ann Davis, Beth Montgomery, Judy Kuipers, Anne Kratz and Anna DiStefano, for their guidance and wonderful conversations; my colleagues at the ICCCR, Morton Deutsch, Peter Coleman, Naira Musallam, Ines Ariceta, Mekayla Castro, Kathryn Crawford, Melissa Sweeney, and Katharina Kugler for giving me your support and allowing me to take the time I needed; my fellow faculty in the Social and Organizational Psychology program at Columbia University, Teachers College, from whom I continue to learn; all the wonderful interculturalists I have met through SIIC and CCTS in Japan, Shoko Araki, Janet Bennett, Milton Bennett, Sheila Ramsey, Dean Barnlund, Mitch Hammer, and more, thank you; and my longtime colleagues Audrey Charlton, Robert Anderson, Carina Stern, and the members of the cross-cultural group who meet regularly to support and learn from each other about the paradoxes of cross-cultural matters.

To my spiritual guides Master Goy, Masami and Hiroo Saionji, I don't know where I would be without you, but it wouldn't be here!

And now it is time for the dormant artist in me to come forward as I engage in the visual arts that have been absent from my life for too long.

## A FEW NOTES OF APPRECIATION FROM KATHY

From my earliest memories, I have always been aware of difference. As a child growing up in Texas in the late 1950s and early 1960s, I remember a time when cultures were segmented and segregated. I have my parents—Samuel and Selma Geller—to thank for teaching me another way of seeing the world, allowing me to query and challenge what I lived and what I saw. To them and to my sister Marilyn Sue Geller, I say "thank you" for providing a foundation of values and the support to "try it all out!"

As Beth wrote, we met almost 12 years ago at Fielding Graduate University. As a mid-career adult, I can think of no experience more powerful than my Doctoral journey. From the first course, where I began to challenge my assumptions and shift my perspective on the world, to the awarding of my degree many years later, this was a life- changing and life-affirming experience. Many people at Fielding were part of my journey. Barbara Mink, Steve Schapiro, and Barnett Pearce offered their wisdom and became strong voices challenging and supporting me during the writing of my dissertation. My continuing work with Barbara and Steve extends and deepens the experience! My Fielding colleagues and now life-long friends—Beth, Jewel Ray-Chaudhuri, Ann Davis, Beth Montgomery, and Kenzie Kwong—continue to offer fascinating conversations, reminding me always of the importance of seeing the world from a range of perspectives.

Living these paradoxes and working from Hong Kong, Kuwait, and Malaysia was made easier by a wide range of friends and colleagues who supported my own development as a transnational leader. My appreciation goes to Thomas Tin-Chak Chen, who in the time of our relationship offered me "the world" (literally), and provided a constant basis for experiencing the paradoxes of transnational leadership 24/7.

To my team in Hong Kong—Rebecca Wai Ting Wong, Spencer Lau, and Eric Chu—you first taught me that "yes" can mean many things and later you showed me the importance of recreating a family in the work setting. I have the greatest admiration for you three and always look forward to our next dinner together.

Just as my work team in Hong Kong offered me a way of knowing myself and appreciating others, my friends in Kuala Lumpur have opened my eyes to the power of living in a multicultural context: to Lili Tan, L.C. Toh, Husnah Wadi, Margaret Sebastian, Sharon Yap and Vanaja Nethi, please know I continue to learn from you in each and every conversation.

For the past four summers, I've had the joy of being a faculty for future school leaders, attending the Columbia University's Summer Principal's Academy. The experience of working with wonderful faculty in a consciously designed transformative learning environment is without comparison. It has been a privilege and journey unto itself to co-teach with Robert Anderson and work with Audrey and Beth. During one of these summers, I can remember a dinner with Jewel and Ray Chaudhuri in New York. I was at a loss on how to communicate effectively with someone in the operations center in Chennai, and Ray offered an insight "from the other end of the continuum" that I had been unable to see through my own lens. It was a magical moment—thank you both!

Across time, distance, and change Donnis Rosenwinkel-Benson remains the most positive person I know, and I thank her for always seeing the rainbow and offering me a glimpse. Priscilla V. Marotta, my best friend for 30 years, continues to be my cheerleader and psychological support, spending time in my homes in Hong Kong and Kuala Lumpur and bringing with her a considered view of alternative frames of reference and perspectives.

To all of you and to others too numerous to list here, thank you for touching my life and offering me new ways to understand the world!

# INDEX

# INDEX

American Management Association
www.amanet.org